Young Writers

CALYPSO

Shropshire & Staffordshire

First published in Great Britain in 1997 by
POETRY NOW YOUNG WRITERS
1-2 Wainman Road, Woodston,
Peterborough, PE2 7BU
Telephone (01733) 230748

All Rights Reserved

Copyright Contributors 1997

HB ISBN 1 86188 375 7
SB ISBN 1 86188 370 6

FOREWORD

Every day, each year the Young Writers' entry sack seems to multiply. Not only do we find the quantity accumulating but progressively we find the standard of young people's poetry growing increasingly eminent.

This is a commendable reflection on authors and English teachers alike. There is no question that a good English teacher produces a good young creative writer, and young people with a passion for poetry are flourishing and at last are being encouraged.

Editing Calypso *Shropshire and Staffordshire* was an editorial nightmare - we found ourselves somewhat spoilt for choice, but thoroughly enjoyed it nonetheless. Featuring poems by young people aged 11-18 years old, some with special needs, the Calypso books contain one of the most diverse ranges of poetry on the market today. Some are complex, emotional and close to the heart, others are simple, light-hearted, and invariably humorous, all demonstrate a good use of language and literary skills. Many illustrate concerns, both socially and environmentally that are fresh in all of our minds. All, I believe, allow the reader access to the minds of today's youth - ultimately proving the power of the pen.

CONTENTS

Abraham Darby School

Andrew Jones	1
Rebecca-Jane Cox	1
Natalie Sutton	2
Emily Jane Lewis	2
Stephanie Moss	3
Nureyev Lanji	4
Sarah Tanner	5
Kathryn Norris	6
Lianne Wright	6
Sarah E Hatton	7
Christine Boden	8

Adams School

Susan Richards	9
John Hughes	9
Hayley Price	10
Lucy Maddocks	10
Christine Rimmer	11
Kathryn Powell	11
Gary France	12
Andrew Dorricott	12
Fiona Scott	13
Sam Bartley	13
Chris Elsmore	14

Bishop's Castle Community College

Fergus Kirkpatrick	14
Jory-Chather	15

Ercall Wood School

Ellen Bellingham	16
Joanne Martin	17
Ben Goh	18
Claire Tipton	19
Michelle Leech	20

Lindsay Cutting	21

Birches Head High School
Katie Edwards	22
Laura Venables	23
Daniel Barcroft	24

City Of Stoke On Trent Sixth Form College
Ben Corden	25

Denstone College
Adrian Crosskey	26
Jennifer Wing	26
Gareth Soar	27
John Wood	28
Nick Hardy	29
Eamon Nawal	30
Barry Green	30
Jade Hurlin	31
Stacey Arland	32
Andrew Pegman	33
James D Edes	34
Victoria Westwood	35
Laura Dexter	36

James Brindley High School
Shaun Brassington	36
Emma Louise Davidson	37
Charlotte Standeven	38
Danielle Kelly	38
Lisa Eardley	39
Samantha Smith	40
Amy Bache	40
Matthew John Byatt	41
Andrew Beech	42
Gemma Aldridge	42
Liam Bailey	43
Louise Castrey	44

Samantha Dearden	44
Martin Foster	45
James Rawlingson	46
Hannah Ward-Salt	46
Adam Webb	47
Michael James Jackson	48
Gavin Hughes	48
Anna Clowes	49

Kingsbury School

Joanne Skidmore	50
Ben Whitehead	51
Ian Thornhill	52
Chris Field	52
Sarah Tonks	53
Ria Mason	54
Kevin Kelly	54
Neil Beasley	55
James Mortimer	56
Sarah Ellis	56
Amy Eaton	57
Clare Marriott	58
Jennifer Bond	59
Ian Davies	60
Adam Cowell	61

Painsley R C High School

Katherine Wilcox	61
Hannah Mason	62
Kathryn Rushton	63
Kerry Lockett	64
Clare Parry	65
Anthony Gamble	66
Alex Durling	67
Owen Griffiths	68
Jennifer Temple-Smith	68
Charles Okell	69
Laura Smith	70

Stewart Fisher	71
Andrew Walton	72
Thomas Dougherty	73
Kathryn Hopkins	74
Emma Cooke	74
Katie May	75
James Lander	75
Jo Alcock	76
Charlotte Hurst	76
Rebecca Brentnall	77
Gavin Stephens	78
Rachel Ayres	79
Sarah Mason	80
Kirsty Hill	81
Lisa Emery	82
Craig Chappell	82
Dominic McDonnell	83
Julia Lund	84

Polesworth High School

Alexandra Somerfield	84
Nathan Askew	85
Helen Birkinshaw	86
Rebecca Byrne	87

Queen Elizabeth's Mercian School

Robyn Catley	88
Anastasia Cassie	88
Sammy England	89
Katie Gilmour	89
Siân Jones	90
Leigh-Anne Barrett	90
David Moore	91
Tom Warrier	91
Dean Sale	92
Laura Brookes	92
Ben Robinson	93
Melanie Veal	94

Sarah Ashwood	94
Aaron Watterson	95
Dan Vallance	95
Steven Deakin	96
Vanessa Higgins	97
Rebecca Jones	98
Lee Marsh	99
Zara Curley	99
Samantha Clements	100
Laura Dolphin	100
Natalie Parboo	101
Kerry Cross	102
Carl Green	103
Louise Griffiths	104
Gareth Lewis	104
Graeme May	105
Natalie Moran	105
Rebecca O'Brien	106
Joanne Parnham	106
Adam Roberts	107
Hannah Bridges	107
Ceri Summers	108
Nicola Watkins	109
Laura Wiggall	109
Suzanne Whitmore	110
Sin Yee Wong	110

Rising Brook High School

Samantha Kennett	111
Geraldine Bradley	111
Suzannah Ecclestone	112
Donna Parsons	112
Lorna Barnett	113
Matthew Long	114
Sarah Thompson	115
Tracey Shore	116
Sally Kendrick	116
Sarah Murray	117

Rocklands School
   Matthew Fletcher   118

St Giles Church of England School
   James Hiam   119

St Thomas More Catholic College
   Katie Mansfield   119
   Dawn Shenton   120
   Adam Rowson   120
   Samantha Housley   121
   Gordon Parton   121
   Amy Day   122
   Philip Bates   122
   Ashley Gouldsmith   123
   Anthony Evans   123
   Sarah Hughes   124
   Samantha Jones   124
   Kirsty Grattage   125
   Simon Carter   125
   Craig Slater   126
   Jenna Wootton   126
   Clare Davis   127
   Paul Storey   128
   Samantha Goodwin   128
   Stephanie Filcock   129
   Lesley Cadman   129
   Rebecca Carrick   130
   Raymond Lam   130
   Robert McGuire   131
   Vicky Davies   131
   Siobhan Daly   132
   Rachel Dawson   133
   Kerrie Evans   133
   Rhian Weston   134
   Fazana Khurshid   134
   Ben Sims   135
   Kieran Bevan   136

Stefan Rouch	136
Isabella Angotti	137
Russell Dimmock	138
Alan Rosenau	138
Simon Dowling	139
Stephen Snee	140
Lianne Jones	140
Clare Parkes	141
Donna Beer	141
Richard Bell	142
Claire Pyatt	142
Isaac Maxwell	143
Steven Booth	143
Russell Ball	144
Dean Quinn	144
Kim Hollins	145
Hayley Miller	146
Dominic Salt	146
Cheryl Smith	147
Matthew Miller	147
Abigail Dodd	148
David Bates	148
Francis Murphy	149
Adam Grannell	150

The Rawlett School

Anne-Marie Boulstridge	151
Mark Dayton	151
Holly Sadler	152
Hannah Martin	152
Sophie Horrobin	153
Annabelle Rowley	153
Marie Jealous	154
Andrew Turner	154
Chris Killeen	155
Mark Demain	156
Jason Reid	157
Sam Collins	157

Rebecca Patten	158
Neil Orton	158
Victoria Masters	159
Andrew Hough	160
Louise Hodgetts	160
Gary Marston	161
Becky Newman	162
Pamela Heafield	162
Simon Griffiths	163
James Allsopp	164
David Gray	165
Ryan McKnight	166
Christopher Soult	166
Jodie Reynolds	167
Lucy Adams	168
Kate Bramwell	168
Gary Thomas	169
Nicholas Malone	170
James Dowen	170
Emma Cardinal	171
Louise Hicks	172
Russell Inglis	172
Shelley Anderton	173
Kieran Eason	173
Sarah Jellema	174
Anna Read	175
Ben Wilkins	175
Dale Lomas	176
Katie Logan	176
Gregg Sadler	177
Fiona McGown	178
Laura Hunt	179
Heather Smith	180
Matthew Hunt	180
Dan Thompson	181
Luke Woollard	182
Nadeem Hussain	183

Trent Valley High School
- Juanita Chatterton — 184
- Casey Wakeman — 184
- Zakia Khan — 185
- Abda Liaget — 186
- Elizabeth Finney — 187
- Jacqueline Beeston — 188
- Samantha Eldridge — 188

Trentham High School
- Matthew Oakes — 189
- Suzanne Byatt — 190
- Laura Beckett — 190
- Felicity Clarke — 191
- Zara Kassai — 192

Weston Road High School
- Katie Williams — 192
- Joanne Emery — 193
- Emily Garner — 194
- Stephanie Wheat — 194
- Lisa Baskeville — 195
- Kathryn Baldwin — 196
- Paul Hayward — 196
- Rachel Ward — 197
- Tamsine Bellaby — 198
- Kylie Godridge — 198
- Grace Elkin — 199
- Ben Doyle — 199
- Gemma Allen — 200
- Sarah Dellar — 200
- Jason Howard — 201
- Abigail Cheshire — 202
- Philippa Valler — 203

Windsor Park Middle School
- Jemma Sellers — 204
- Ashley Roe — 204

Andrew Woodings	205
Nadia Nijim	205
Helen Crump	206
James Brazendale	206
Caroline Williams	207
Justine Locker	208
Graham Langridge	209
Steven Kerry	210
Helen Wilson	211
Connie Corbishley	211
Hayley Goodwin	212
Kelly Staley	212
Andrew Aitken	213
Lyndi Thompson	213
Kate Backhouse	214
Sarah Turner	215
Vicky Bailey	216

THE POEMS

A Night In The Graveyard

My friend with me, creeping through the graveyard
Full moon in the sky, church steeple towering high.
My friend with me, frightened in the graveyard
It's Hallowe'en tonight, and the full moon's shining bright.
My friend with me, saw ghosts in the graveyard
Demons all around, we fell onto the ground.
My friend with me, screaming in the graveyard
Suddenly the sound: church bells ring aloud.
My friend with me, dashing through the graveyard
We stopped dead in our tracks, werewolves behind our backs.

Andrew Jones (11)
Abraham Darby School

As I Looked Through

As I looked through my window,
To behold the sunset.
I saw the colour it had,
The scarlet, rosy-pink red,
The golden - orange.
As bright as shiny brass,
And the shining bright meadow yellow.
All this reflecting off the fluffy white clouds.

As I looked through my window,
I saw the open fields of grass.
The apple green emerald grass,
Fields and fields of it,
Gleaming in the beautiful day sun.

Rebecca-Jane Cox (11)
Abraham Darby School

Dolphins!

I see them there,
Swimming through the vast deep.
The glistening blue,
Water as clear as can be.

With the waves so uneven,
As the dolphins jump through them.
With their neutral grey skin,
That's so slippery it's like ice.

They move so gracefully,
Fast and free like volcanoes.
Just waiting to erupt,
Because they're so excited.

How I wish I could swim with them,
Through the vast deep.
Some day I will I know I will,
Let's just hope that day comes true.

Natalie Sutton (11)
Abraham Darby School

Rocket

I lay in bed dreaming.
A dream I wish could come true.
I dream of a black horse,
Running wild and free.

As he gallops towards me,
His tail and mane are like black silk,
His eyes are like black beads,
Looking straight at me.

Over the rippling field he runs.
Elegant and graceful he moves.
He is like a rocket,
Hooves tapping and clapping on the ground.

Here I am dreaming,
But how I wish my dream
Would come true,
I wish he was mine.

Emily Jane Lewis (11)
Abraham Darby School

VOLCANOES

The orange and red lava bursting out
The colours of a rainbow never peep out.
While the earth is splitting,
The lava is spitting.
The running people who have nowhere to go
The rage of the lava still bubbling below.
The shouting, and screaming of the volcano's eruption
The village below is near to destruction.
Lava burst out colours orange and red
As it runs down the mountain to the village ahead.
Panic emerges from, young and old,
Unable to take in the destruction that will unfold.
The darkness of night looms ahead
'It's the end of the world,' people have said.
Of all the destruction the volcano has caused
The disturbance, the screaming has now paused.
The happy life in this village before,
Is now devastation to one and all.

Stephanie Moss (11)
Abraham Darby School

WHALES

As I go down to the ocean
The sun beats down on the sea,
I see ripples
Like waves!
Then look,
I see something like a big black blanket,
I look closer then I realise,
A whale!
He jumped out of the water and back in,
The splash was like a waterfall crashing in the sea.

A ship came by with a gun
To shoot the whale,
A little squirt of water came out of his breathing hole,
But the man didn't care,
He shot him.

I saw the whale being free,
Now all I see is red, red for blood.

When I see make-up in the shop,
I remember the whale shot
For powder on our faces,
Lipsticks on our lips.

Nureyev Lanji (11)
Abraham Darby School

My Diary

My secrets are safe
And locked away tight,
Hidden under my pillow
Out of sight.

My diary is small
Tatty and torn,
Everything has been noted
Since the day I was born.

The lock is fixed tight
And secured in a dark cupboard at night,
With my teddy bears alert,
Ready to fight.

My daydreams are noted down
With a date by their side,
Just in case one day I achieve
That long adventurous journey ride.

Still clutching my key so safe
Next to me,
Just in case like a secret agent
I have to flee.

Sarah Tanner (11)
Abraham Darby School

MY LOST DOG

It's bonfire night,
My charcoal dog is so scared;
He can't move,
My hairy, scary dog has disappeared,
Into the night.

When will bonfire night end?
One more bang,
My dog has gone,
Gone, gone, gone.

Bonfire night has gone again,
Disappeared for another year.
But still my poor dog,
Has not returned.

My scary dog came back to me,
All frightened and shivering, to death,
His hair sticking up on end.
Crying out for me,
He is so scared he is fading away,
Away, away, away.

Kathryn Norris (11)
Abraham Darby School

DOLPHIN

I walk, walk up to the shore
Watching the waves, hearing them roar
I see something jumping at sea
I see a dolphin the dolphin sees me

The dolphin leaps as it plays
In and out over the waves
The dolphin splashes out at sea
I wish we could swim, dolphin and me

I stepped, stepped into the sea
Oh it's cold, as cold as can be
Finally I got to swim, with the dolphin
I touched, touched its lovely silky skin

I touched the bottom of the sea
We make a great pair the dolphin and me
It's time, time for me to go
And maybe we could, also swim tomorrow.

Lianne Wright (11)
Abraham Darby School

THE SKELETON

Scary, skeleton,
Crawling along the downstairs hall
Standing straight looking sinister and tall

Crawling up the stairs,
Coming to get me.
Crawling up the door,
Coming to get me.

Creepy skeleton opening my door,
Moaning and groaning even more.
I open my eyes, sweat running down
my head.
Thank God no skeleton by my bed!

Sarah E Hatton (11)
Abraham Darby School

My Darling Pony

Even though you've left me,
Even though you've gone,
I'd just like to tell you,
My memories linger on.

You're still remembered clearly,
But you could hardly carry on,
Your bright face was dulling,
The end was dragging on.

I loved the way you galloped,
Up the field to meet me,
The wind was blowing fast,
Your hooves were beating hard.

The times we had together,
Made it hard for us to part.
But your condition was heartbreaking,
And that was just the start.

A cure could be found.
There may have been a chance,
But while we were searching,
The days were running out.

Your bay fur was so shiny.
Your mane was so black.
Your blue eyes were so sparkling,
Your white blaze was so bright.

Goodbye my darling pony,
I hope you're happy there,
Forever I will miss you,
If only you'd be there.

Christine Boden (12)
Abraham Darby School

THE QUEEN

A butterfly flying around,
Painted so delicately,
In pink, brown and blue,
If you would be a letter you would be S
For slender silk and smiley.
Your season is May,
and your day is Tuesday.

With photographers clicking,
on their cameras now I know why you smile.

You get chased but you win,
Always calm and collected.
With blue and red flags swishing in the wind.
You're bright and perky,
in your big cocoon.
With flowers to match your colours.

Susan Richards (12)
Adams School

ANDREI KANCHELSKIS

Kanchelskis is the speed of lightning,
He's a cheetah darting past defenders,
A rocket into orbit.
In his blue shirt dazzling in the bright sun.
He's letter silky S for skill, colour red for danger,
and as sharp as a machete by the throat.
He eyes a space and uses his skills like silk,
Unstoppable like a runaway mine train.
Strikes the ball as fast as a speeding bullet,
It cracks the bar and trickles over the line,
The crowd cheer as loud as a roaring lion.

John Hughes (11)
Adams School

BON JOVI

He's a *werewolf* at 1am in the
morning howling through the night.

He's like *vodka* because he's so *hot*.

He's like a *rubber* so bendable and
flexible.

He's a *gobstopper* all sweet and hard.

He's the colour of *black*.

He's a *snake* sly and sneaky.

He's the letter *S* for *Superman* coming
to save me.

Hayley Price (12)
Adams School

GAZZA

His piercing blue eye looking at me
A fiery F in the alphabet
Calling his cat food Gazza's Great Grub
He's a white rose the colour of his hair
A down-to-earth darting fly
He's a wild polar bear with speed and grace
The joker of the pack
An iron man brilliant player on the pitch
A blue bouncing ball
He's milky warm tea
A hoppy rabbit when he scores.

Lucy Maddocks (12)
Adams School

RONAN KEATING

He's a bird of prey ready to pounce,
Hypnotising his prey with his narrow eyes.
His spiky hair like a porcupine,
Too dangerous to touch.
His singing is soft and comforting,
Ready to wipe you off your seat.
Every Sunday in December,
Beware! This is his best day.
His favourite letter of the alphabet,
Is *V* for *victory* over people.
In his spare time,
Rich Tea biscuits are what he likes eating best.
His favourite colour,
Is blue for the sky.

Christine Rimmer (11)
Adams School

PETER ANDRE

He's a hunk of gods, with his muscly chest,
He's a big scary panther with his fierce eyes,
He's a big lovely Bacardi and Coke,
His night would be Saturday.
He's a nice sweet smell,
He's a big juicy pineapple tree,
His colour would be red.
His letter is L in the alphabet,
He looks like a Swiss roll,
His month is April.
He dances like a flame of fire,
He sings like a beam of sun lighting up the day.

Kathryn Powell (11)
Adams School

Eric Cantona

He's fierce like a lion and
skilful like a monkey.
He's strong like He-Man in
action.
Eric is the colour red for
danger.
And he's the letter F for
fierce.
When he charges up field
he's like a bull chasing
someone.
He's Wednesday in the week,
and autumn in the seasons.
In his bright red shirt
running up centre field
taking on defenders shooting
and scoring.
He's a red hot balti and a
strong red wine.

Gary France (11)
Adams School

Eric Cantona

There is a man called Cantona
who everyone knows as a star
His sport is football
and when his team hears his call
that ball goes in the net
The crowd knows it's the best
and shout ooh ah
Cantona

Andrew Dorricott (12)
Adams School

FATHER CHRISTMAS

Look carefully through the blizzard and you might see
A bright rosy candle in the winter cold.
A winter comer, hibernating in the summer,
The Christmas spirit, telling everyone it's Christmas time.

A big cuddly bear-cub inside an aged shell,
Like a child, but full of knowledge.
A booming bassoon with elves for percussion,
The elves' delicate jingle, his hearty cries.
A pair of scissors, cutting through the night sky in his sleigh.

A hearty fire with tufts of snow,
A twinkling eye, a bright old smile,
A heart of gold, with plenty of padding to protect it.

Fiona Scott (11)
Adams School

ERIC CANTONA

He's a thunderbolt charging down the pitch in a danger *red* T-shirt
A tiger darting in and out of players.
Wishing he was British as he shoots.

He waves a hand at the crowd as the ball hits the net he's like a gold medallist.
The *Reds* come from all directions congratulating the mighty one.
His day would be a Saturday, partying.
He's like a glass of red wine celebrating
His biscuit would be a shortbread.

Sam Bartley (11)
Adams School

DENNIS BERGKAMP

D arts around the pitch.
E veryone can't catch him up.
N obody can tackle him.
N obody, he's a brilliant player.
I t's a manager's pleasure to have him.
S upporters love him.

B ergkamp darts through the players.
E veryone challenges him but it won't work
R unning around the pitch.
G oing crazy around the pitch.
K is for kind like a sharing boy.
A calm player
M any people think he's good.
P eople are fans of his.

Chris Elsmore (11)
Adams School

WOLF CRY

As I walk in the crunching snow
I can hear a church bell ring
The trees wave in a howling wind
The lights from a house fade away.

The river is fast yet unheard
You can hear the cry of the wolves
The pounding paws on the hard frozen ground
Can be heard from the mountains so high.

The approaching sound of barking
A bloodthirsty cry from above
There are eyes in the trees
And they're looking at me for
I am their warm winter meal.

Fergus Kirkpatrick (12)
Bishop's Castle Community College

LONGMYND HILL

Longmynd Hill,
It used to contain a mill.
A silent breeze running through your hair,
I seem to be the only one who can care.
The sun blazing down,
Up here you wear the crown.
Picnics are on,
Right now I'm eating a scone.
Hang-gliding high in the sky,
People shouting
I can fly
Birds flying,
Nothing's dying
The place is full of sheep.
Excuse me while,
I'm going to sleep.

Jory-Chather (12)
Bishop's Castle Community College

OUR FATHER!

When he died,
I always cried,
It was a lot of pain,
I couldn't take the strain.

It was like a clash of thunder,
He was 6ft under,
I cannot see without him,
There's a shadow in my path.

I loved him, he loved me,
Can it still be
My heart is like the world,
Only there's a segment missing.

My mind is like the weather,
You don't know what's happening next,
I always thought he was clever,
Now I'll never know.

My feelings are mixed,
My thoughts are scrambled,
I do something wrong,
I know he is watching.

The way it was then,
I know it will never be,
Oh father I love you,
I wish you could see me.

I look at your pictures,
They are not as good,
I wish I could see you
in the flesh and blood,
I know I never could.

Sorry to let you go
Rest in peace.

Ellen Bellingham (15)
Ercall Wood School

THE BULLY

My friends,
I didn't know they had it in them.
What had I done.
Nothing.

I didn't know so many names existed.
When they stood in front of me.
The whole playground was empty.
I was alone.

The names came thick and fast,
But I just couldn't tell.
What made it worse was that
They were in my class.

The weekend was worse,
I couldn't go to school.
Eventually I told.
My teacher said 'Sticks and stones may break my bones
But names will never hurt me'
But they did.

Joanne Martin (14)
Ercall Wood School

MY TRAIN

Seven oh-nine - been waiting since half-six;
My old beauty'll be coming round the corner pretty soon.
A Saturday well spent. The cold, damp concourse,
Spattered with chewing gum, old vomit. Pretty soon,
She'll be coming.

Nine twenty-six - the cool air, clear.
I can sense old Annie near.
The wilting hanging baskets; life spent long ago,
A death of waiting for their train to come.
I can hear her.

Ten fifty-three - an announcement cuts the air.
The pigeons flutter and fly from the nests,
The ground below them, a black and white bomb site.
A contrasting pellet bombards my jotter.
Pretty soon, pretty soon.

Noon - will she come for me?
Another hour or so, I'll stay my time . . .
She's here! Her old, tired lights slide
Under the bridge.
My frozen, sausage fingers writhe for my biro.

She's in front of me.
Her windows' dust and cluttered grease,
Cut by 'Goff woz ere'.
My eyes search,
For my long-coming prize;
The 7.16 from Euston, 82157.
Tick.
Twelve oh-five - a train's a comin'.

Ben Goh (15)
Ercall Wood School

BULLYING

Bullying is wrong
people get hurt
name calling, stealing
that always comes first.

Physically, emotionally, mentally too
think twice before you do it, it could happen to you

Bullies go round
in groups thinking they're hard
ask 'em for a fight
and you might be alright.

Physically, emotionally, mentally too
think twice before you do it, it could happen to you

Walking out my house
thinking why
tell me, tell me
I don't want to die

Physically, emotionally, mentally too
think twice before you do it, it could happen to you

So if you're getting bullied
tell someone
having it done to you
is not much fun

Physically, emotionally, mentally too
I've now stopped my bullying, and so should you.

Claire Tipton (14)
Ercall Wood School

CRUEL WORLD

The world was created for everyone to share,
Racism and violence should be stripped bare.
All cultures and beliefs should be treated right,
It's not fair that people always fight.

Women and men should be equal and free,
Then we'll all be happy, it'll be easy to see.
Greed should be thrown far away from this planet,
Sexism should be stopped, so why don't we ban it?

What is wrong with the world, tell me now,
End all of the unhappiness, but the problem is how.
The world is an ugly and violent place,
And now it's reflecting on the human race.

There is no way of having a happy life,
Because we have to live with nothing but strife.
Stop it now, there's no reason why,
Some people find it funny seeing others die.

Wars threaten and end people's lives,
There's no reason why we have to hear their cries.
Leave the world, let it be free,
Then we'll all be happy, you just wait and see.

Michelle Leech (14)
Ercall Wood School

REGRETS

Regretting it
Why, why that word runs over and over again in
my mind.
Someone said it was funny,
Some said nothing happens to you,
While others said it gives you a buzz.
I was curious, too curious for my own good.
Consequences never crossed my selfish mind,
Curiosity killed the cat.
Anger, frustration, stupid, stupid girl.
I only did it once, 30 seconds it lasted.
Now everything I've ever worked for has gone,
No trust, no respect, no nothing!
I'm a nobody.
Was it worth it?
They said it was legal, who knows?
I was lucky, extremely lucky.
Drugs are for losers, let it be a lesson,
It's one I'll never forget.

Lindsay Cutting (15)
Ercall Wood School

WAR

Monstrous machines, explosives and screams,
bombs soar and roar in the sky.
Whizzes, whooshes, incendiaries and crashes,
accidents, blood, death and crying.

Guns, tanks, maniacs and soldiers,
bullets fired in every direction,
like a firework display on bonfire night.
Screaming people running down the half
erupted street.

Why all this pain and hatred for selfish,
greedy people?
The population decreasing day by day,
with nothing to be gained.

Bombs explode maiming innocent people,
every day and every night.
Hurtful words shouted from a person without
any need at all.

Why do people do this?
It's a question that needs to be answered.

Katie Edwards (13)
Birches Head High School

NOT AGAIN

I'm all alone, away from him,
trying to be brave.
Scared and lonely waiting for him,
to strike another blow.

I'm waiting, frozen to the spot,
is that him now?
I've done nothing wrong,
Please God help me.

Oh no! He's here, back from his work,
Probably another bruise to match the others.
The pain, it hurts, aching so much,
what can I do? He's so strong.

I hate him so, I really do,
big, brutal and petrifying.
His eyes are evil, his voice is cold,
how can I stop him? I'm scared.

He's climbing the stairs, his feet so loud,
he's opened the door, it's too late to run.
My chin starts to quiver, I'm so afraid,
one, two, three, *bang!* I'm on the floor.

He's gone back again, downstairs,
leaving me to my wounds.
Blood again, I'm not surprised,
please God help me.

Laura Venables (13)
Birches Head High School

MISSING

They're *missing*, gone
Innocents, playing, lost in a world of wonder.
The sky turned black and rumbled with thunder.
Buckets and spades, footprints all gone.
Parents busy, oh what a blunder.

Their job all done! They looked up.
In a blink of the eye, where are they?
Names shouted, cries of anguish, 'where are you?'
Beach deserted, hours pass by, they search in vain.
Looking at the mother, you could see she was in pain.

Passers by stopped in panic, help us please.
The mother was seen begging at her knees.
Plea and a prayer to God she sent.
Where are my children, she makes her pleas.
And the father stares out in wonder at the seas.

Days gone by, not a sound heard.
The mother braces herself for those fatal words.
She turned grey faced and hoped she hadn't heard.
The hope of finding them alive, like a flickering candle.
And if they're not, oh what a burden for the mother to handle.

The mother listens and her worries are now over.
The children found dead, buried in each other's arms.
The mother identifies the bodies, she puts their grey cold hands in her palms.
She is deeply saddened and faints in despair.
The father stops and thinks about the rotten affair.

It all ended in disarray
One fatal family fun beach day.

Daniel Barcroft (13)
Birches Head High School

PENSIVE POINT

What damned world is this
        Where thinking brings us sorrow?
Where newly blossomed notions
        Have wilted by tomorrow?

At first the thoughts are pleasing,
        They clear up the sky,
Content clouds float sedately,
        Serene - my mind and I.

But I look at every angle,
        A dizzy bird in flight,
No joy in seeing the sunrise
        Then immediately, the night.

Soon the clouds are bulging
        As dark mists rise again,
Soon the clouds are bursting,
        Mind aches from pounding rain!

Thought smashes into thought
        And they beat against the bay,
Passions are extinguished
        And life is washed away.

The mind ascends the body,
        Confused clouds meet hand in hand,
The storm knocks me senseless -
        A stupor in the sand.

Ben Corden (16)
City Of Stoke On Trent Sixth Form College

THE SIBLING

It's called Sib, short for sibling,
With her hair dyed like plums,
Her lean face, with blue eyes,
And unworn hands, used for nothing but love,
Apart from when I annoy her.
Then she digs her long painted, nails,
Just above my wrist,
Where my veins stick out,
so I bleed and it hurts.
She is clever while I am vacuous,
Her best friend is a year ahead,
But mine is behind,
She is two and a half years older than me,
But I am still taller than her,
She is about five feet three inches,
Which is pretty small for her age,
When the rest of her class are nearly six feet.
But even though Sib hurts me I
still love her because,
Sib is my sister.

Adrian Crosskey (13)
Denstone College

THE GIRL

I recall looking at her lean ashen face,
Her conspicuous pouted lips giving her a sultry appearance,
She moves with sprightliness and grace,
Her frail body moving at steady pace.

A mass of tight coarse curls,
Cascaded down her back,
Like a rippling sheet,
The chestnut glow was scarcely discreet

She delicately brushed her hair with her fingers
Cautious and attentive.
Showing her glittering eyes of a tender hue
And as she laughed they shone a
                distinct azure blue.

Her face broadened as she smiled,
Exposing her sparkling pearl teeth,
Her dimpled cheeks, red,
Combined exquisitely with her square,
                shaped head.

Jennifer Wing (14)
Denstone College

DAVID

David is twelve years of age,
He has short brown curly hair,
Big brown beady eyes,
And bright white shiny teeth,
A cheeky, chubby and smiley face.
He is short in build and has small feet.
He has short stubby fingers on small hands.
He is very bright and clever,
And is a good sports player.
He makes me happy with his cheeky
and chirpy sense of humour.
He sometimes gets mad with me,
But he makes me happy because
he is fun to be with.

Gareth Soar (13)
Denstone College

HIM

Short blonde hair above blue eyes
Surrounded by a dark blue frame,
Clipped onto two lobeless ears.
His left hand drawn and gnarled,
Awaiting treatment by the NHS,
Collared shirt with jeans and sweater,
Is his student wear.
As a B Ed he tries to gain,
To become a teacher with glory and fame.
His voice is used to great effect,
Whether school rugby or football it's at
Full humour and laughter loud,
We very rarely sit under a cloud,
Unless at golf he's played below par,
Then black gloom envelops all.
His work and sport is his love,
As well as his family.
He commentates on football matches,
Even though he's at home.
If he does well at college,
Or his football team wins,
The house gets filled with light,
As he tells us about his day.

John Wood (13)
Denstone College

My Old Friend!

A little like me, my friend of old,
Not as tall, but hair of gold,
Sport is a must,
Rugby team or bust,
Sometimes angry sometimes pleasant,
Always clever and effervescent,
Small squat nose on a freckled face,
All is ruined by that awful brace,
Friend of old no longer near,
We lost touch at the end of the year,
Old school tie, with never a moan,
Would always help without a groan,
My old friend is missed, alas,
Perhaps we'll meet when our lives have passed,
Maybe then we'll still be friends,
Our friendship will never end,
When we've both grown old and grey,
Maybe then one special day,
We'll meet and talk about our lives,
Talk about our children and our wives,
The talk we'll have about all we've missed,
All the talks that I will list,
And keep them till another time,
All the fun we'll share over a bottle of wine.

Nick Hardy (13)
Denstone College

My Mum

She has cared for me,
Brought me up when my
Father passed away.
My mum.
She cares for me all the time,
When I'm ill she makes me well,
When I'm tired she makes it quiet.
My mum.
Flowing brown hair and a
Flowery dress,
Smiling face and golden bracelets.
Always beautiful in my eyes.
My mum.
Always there when you need her
Most.
My mum.
Kind and caring, loving and
Gentle, soft and soothing.

Eamon Nawal (13)
Denstone College

People

Six foot five with short brown hair,
Cropped close to the skull,
His hair short, his head almost bare,
He cuts it himself, people say it looks dull.

Aged twenty-two he knows it all,
Tall and proud,
They say pride comes before a fall,
But then, he has never gone with the crowd.

My brother unique, standing alone,
Even with others he is all too obvious,
In everything he shines,
Jealousy beckons.

His intended he loves, too much to behold,
While his family he forsakes, stays far away,
My mother, distraught, when she was told,
Because deep down she wants him to stay.

Barry Green (13)
Denstone College

THE GIRL

Her long golden hair shines in the sunlight,
Her young skin glows soft and tight.

The tips of her toes splash in the sparkly stream,
Her eyes wander as if in a daydream.

The clouds overhead make shadows on her face,
She sits still anytime, any place.

Her gentle hands are placed in her lap,
Her dainty finger makes a quiet tap tap.

She sits on her own watching the world go by,
She takes a deep breath and lets out a sigh.

Her brilliant blue eyes match the sky,
As she looks up, to watch a bird fly.

Time passes, light sinks away,
Now there is no time to play.

Jade Hurlin (13)
Denstone College

DREAM LOVER

I looked into his large, beady eyes,
They were as blue as the heavenly skies.
His hair is the colour of sand by the sea,
It whirled in the wind, soft and free.
The stubble on his chin
Showed up his firm, taut skin.
The button nose in the centre of his face
Is outlined with a thin trace.
Those distinct lips, as red as a rose,
Surely match his dainty nose.

His angelic face, built on broad shoulders,
Makes his body like a large boulder.
The well-built body, strong and tall,
Then the deepened sound of his call.
Following that comes a cheerful laugh,
Boyish I know, but I'm sure he's tough.
And with his extended chest
He has to be the very best.

Next, I heard him clomping down the hall,
I was so faint I thought I would fall.
There's him, with a radiant look,
And here's me, standing with a book.
I felt so stupid in my cotton shirt,
Matching that, my long grey skirt.
And there was him, wearing designer jeans,
Not bad, for a boy in his teens.
One day I dream we'll kiss,
He'll be mine and I'll be his.

Stacey Arland (13)
Denstone College

MY UNCLE

I know a man with great personality,
Cheerful looks and short brown hair,
He has a happy mouth and creases by his
eyes because he smiles,
And his facial expressions show that he has
a great joking flair.

I know a man who has two amicable children,
Two daughters they are, one aged one and one aged three,
When he is around they have a great time.

He speaks with a Yorkshire accent,
Shouting out loud, whilst running down the rugby
pitch with a ball, knocking people flat to the floor.

But that's a game,
He would never do that in real life,
He is too kind,
He cares for people too much, to do that sort of thing.

He's a great bloke,
He has good times and he has bad times,
But, because of his talents, manages to make
most of them good.

Andrew Pegman (14)
Denstone College

HIM

That's him over there,
With his strangled white hair,
Him, the chubby one,
He usually wears a hat,
Red at that.
He's lost three fingers,
He says they ache when the frost is around.
He's one of those people,
Who is always joking
And other times he acts *deadly serious*.
He's a stubby person,
With a big head.
His nose is enormous,
Only joking,
It's actually quite small,
But you only see hair in that area,
Pouring out of his nostrils,
It's disgusting.
His great big eyes staring round,
Blue and black,
From when he got robbed.
Now he just works in his garden.

James D Edes (13)
Denstone College

My Grandma

Her wrinkly skin and weather-beaten face
Give my grandma her distinctiveness
She's warm and kind and full of cheer
Her snowy white hair and bony fingers
Remind me of a skeleton.
But even though on the outside
She looks old and weary,
Inside her heart she's as young as me
When she smiles her eyes light up
Like stars on a dark night.
I love the way she loves to talk
About when she was young
And the things she did.
And the way her hands move
Swiftly over the soft linen
As she makes her clothes
A hobby she enjoys so much
But most of all I love her
A woman so full of knowledge and generosity
And a person who is always there
When you need them.

Victoria Westwood (13)
Denstone College

GRANDMOTHER

When she smiles her worn face
Gently folds into soft lines
Her smile turns into a laugh
Her sea mist eyes suddenly turn sad
The laughter fades from her face
She looks down at the pattern of shapes and colours
She has cleverly sewn together with her experienced hands
She stands up and walks towards the buzzing
A lovely smell fills the air
The smell of a freshly baked pie
She walks out of the kitchen then back in
To and fro, into the garden
Artfully scattering buds of life into the chocolate ground
When she comes inside she sits down
She leans forward and fiddles with flowers
Changing them making them look wonderful
She then goes back to her knitting
She looks up and her whole face smiles at me
I smile back.

Laura Dexter (14)
Denstone College

RUNNING татTo The Finish Line

Running to the finish line
Sprinting from the starting line
Speeding up all the time
Your heart can't stop beating
The wind is blowing in your face
You have got to carry on
And finish the race to get
A place in the final run.

Shaun Brassington (11)
James Brindley High School

Day Dreaming

Mrs Robinson thinks I'm reading
But I'm not . . .
I'm in a famous play,
Or on a tropical island,
Lying on the beach,
With servants at my side,
I'm on the moon,
Jumping up and down,
'Wake up!' and it's back to reality

My Mum thinks I'm washing up.
But I'm not . . .
I'm in a magic show,
Spinning plates,
Then it's on to the moon
It's made of chocolate,
Yum! Yum!
Crash!
Oh! No! My Mum's best china
I'm in trouble

My sister thinks I'm listening,
But I'm not . . .
I'm at the zoo taming tigers,
I'm in a room full of chocolate,
I'm in a snow fight,
In my street
All the family at Alton Towers
Are you listening to me?
'Oh! Sorry!'

Emma Louise Davidson (11)
James Brindley High School

CAVING

The shiver down my back gave me the creeps.
The cave was gloomy
And scary.
I didn't know what was going to happen next,
When suddenly
We turned the lights out.
Oh! No!
Crawling through the worm squirm gave me
The creeps.
It got tighter
And tighter
Then lower
And lower.
The darkness was gaining
It got colder
And colder
Then suddenly, the shiver went down my back again.
All I could hear was the dripping water.
The smell was different.
We are nearly at the end
                At last . . .

Charlotte Standeven (11)
James Brindley High School

THE WITCH'S SPELL

The witch's spell
was hard to make,
But not for her,
This is what she'd take.

She'd take the eyes,
From little kids
And frogs' legs from the
nearest lakes.

Snakes and lizards,
here and there,
She'd even add some of
her hair,
The witch's spell,
Will soon be done
This is all she needs
But more.

Danielle Kelly (11)
James Brindley High School

SPRING

Spring is such a wonderful season,
It makes me want to sing,
The new seeds start to shoot,
And little flowers appear,
The blossom on the trees,
Is such a wonderful sight,
The new-born lambs stand close to their mothers
Eating the fresh green grass,
The little birds return
From their winter flight,
Singing as they build
Their little nests
For their little families,
The leaves on the trees,
All turn green,
Instead of yellow, orange or none at all,
In the distance you will see
The first spring sunset,
Far far away,
Going behind the hills,
Ready for another day.

Lisa Eardley (11)
James Brindley High School

WINTER'S AROUND THE CORNER

Winter's in the air,
You can tell it's everywhere,
The birds are going,
And the north wind's blowing.

The snow will surely come,
And then we can have some fun,
We can have a snowball fight,
Or make a snowman to last all night.

The lakes are frozen over with ice,
It's safe for us to skate round it twice,
When the snow and ice begin to thaw,
I won't be sad because I know there'll be more.

Samantha Smith (11)
James Brindley High School

NIGHT SKY

When the sun goes down
The night sky goes up:
The stars look like fireflies
And blackness sweeps over the sky

When the moon is full,
It looks like a man:
You can only see it when there's a clear sky
All those miles away.

The darkness is like a blanket
Covering the city:
But we're in bed
So we don't see
The night sky.

Amy Bache (11)
James Brindley High School

THE GIANT

I was on a walk with friends,
Through the Scottish hills and glens,
When one of my friends said 'Stop what's that?'
So I lifted the beak of my hat.

And there before my eyes stood one
So mighty I was overcome:
A giant, yes, no more, no less;
My friends and I stood in distress!

One of my friends said 'Hello!'
The giant said 'You should go,
Before I eat you for tea!
It will be a tasty snack, don't you agree?'

One of my friends had a cunning plan,
'Let's go quick before he puts us in the frying pan,
We better run fast or it will be too late,
He will have us on his dinner plate.'

So we won't go up there never,
Or it might be our last day *ever,*
It's better for us to stay at home,
And those there glens we shall never roam.

Matthew John Byatt (11)
James Brindley High School

Football Crazy

The strikers always shoot,
With their big expensive boots.
Cantona he never rests,
Because of course he's just the best.
Natural skills on the ball,
And the ability to thrill all.
Really jazzy football shoes,
Weird celebrations too.
The referees never seem fair
They really shouldn't ever be there.
So you see I'm football crazy, like so many others,
And sadly I haven't any football crazy brothers.

Andrew Beech (11)
James Brindley High School

The Snowflakes

Snowflake, snowflake:
Falling to the ground
Snowflake, snowflake:
Now you are down

Soon I'll come out
To play in the snow
And all of my friends
Will play with me too.

Snowflake, snowflake:
Where are you?
Snowflake, snowflake:
It's half-past two.

Gemma Aldridge (11)
James Brindley High School

The First Day

August!
The football season's here
And
The crowds get ready to cheer
For the teams they love so dear.
3 o'clock!
It's kick-off time,
The season has begun
Newcastle v Wimbledon,
Through the tunnel the players will run.
The manager's in the dugout,
Sitting anxiously
As the player steps up to take a penalty.
Bang!
It's in the net.
So Newcastle win their first game,
Other teams won too,
Who will win the Premiership?
Nobody's got a clue.
My favourite team made a draw today
But that doesn't matter at all,
Although they didn't win,
I'd still support them,
Even if they couldn't kick a ball.

Liam Bailey (11)
James Brindley High School

Autumn

Leaves fall,
Winds blow,
People hurry,
Sun gets low.

Nights grow long,
Days grow cold,
Fog swirls around,
People young and old.

New mornings come,
With layers of frost,
As autumn arrives,
And summer is lost.

Louise Castrey (11)
James Brindley High School

My Environment

Walking in the countryside
On an autumn evening
The air so sweet and clean and crisp.
A lot of wonderful things to see on that cheerful
evening.
The leaves changing colour falling from
the trees.
Well I can't paint so I have to take
my camera.
I capture the beautiful things around me.
Look at trees and say what wonderful
things they are.
I try to name them but I
forget what they are.

Samantha Dearden (13)
James Brindley High School

Manchester United

Man Utd has a famous player,
Ryan Giggs is his name,
He kicks the ball, he scores the goals,
That's how you play the game.

Another one is Cantona,
When he blushes he goes red,
He's also good at football,
But enjoys kicking people in the head.

Schmeichel plays in the goals,
Peter is his first name,
The opposition kicks the ball, he saves the ball,
That's how he plays the game.

Alex Ferguson is the manager,
He bosses them about,
If they fall behind in a match,
You'd hear him swear and shout.

Manchester United,
Are the greatest team by far,
Every single player
Is an international star.

Martin Foster (11)
James Brindley High School

THE COLD NIGHT

In the middle of the cold, dark night.
Strange shadows and noises give me such a fright.
My teeth chatter, my knees wobble.
My little nose looks like a bobble.
My brother's on the bottom bunk,
Feel the shivers, sounds like a funk.
The floorboards creak, the door knob rattles,
I hide my face under my pillow,
There's a shadow on the wall but O, thank God it's just a willow.

James Rawlingson (11)
James Brindley High School

IN A FAR-AWAY TOWN

In a far-away town
Nobody knows you.

'Another stranger,' they say.

Forever staring,
And never caring,
Really upset me today.

Another stranger passes.
Why does no-one speak?
Another stranger passes,
You float by on the street.

Together you're ignoring me,
Oh you're really boring me,
Why does everyone walk?
Never stopping to talk.

Hannah Ward-Salt (11)
James Brindley High School

ME

Are you looking at me?
Tell me, what do you see?
    A number in a book?
    Take a closer look,
    A name on a list?
    Is there something you've missed?
    A face in a crowd?
    For crying out loud!
Look closer, see *me*.

I am a person with feelings,
    With family and friends,
    With hobbies and interests,
Can you not see?

I have emotions, both high and low,
    Triumphs and anxieties,
    Fears and woe,
Now do you see?

The highs are good,
    And there are many,
Like scoring the winner
    Worth a pretty penny.

The lows are bad,
    And thankfully few,
Like losing the championship,
    What *did* I do?

Is the picture getting clearer?
Now what do you see?
Do you see a person?
If so, that's *me!*

Adam Webb (11)
James Brindley High School

SISTERS

My sisters are silly,
silly like me.
Silly and stupid,
as daft as can be.

My sisters they shout,
usually at me.
They shout in the morning,
they shout at tea.

My sisters like boys,
but they don't like me.
I've seen them kissing boys,
but they don't kiss me.

My sisters are older,
older than me.
When one was five,
the other was three.

My sisters they argue,
mostly with me.
But I still love them,
I hope they love me.

Michael James Jackson (12)
James Brindley High School

A WINTER'S TALE

The summer's been
The summer's gone
The winter's here
It's just begun.

Winter is here, it's bitter cold
Frost on the windows
Frost on my toes.

Rainy days and rainy nights
Oh I miss that summer time.

Snow on the roofs
Snow on the ground
Not a blue sky to be found.

Winter's nearly done
Waiting for summer and lots of fun.

Gavin Hughes (12)
James Brindley High School

ENDANGERED ANIMALS

The big grey elephant,
The chimpanzee,
Why people hunt them,
I fail to see.

I want them all back,
With pandas and bats,
But one thing I lack,
Is a pat on the back.

People don't see,
What harm they can cause,
Their callousness and thoughtlessness,
If only they would pause,
To think of these animals,
Instead of themselves.

Anna Clowes (13)
James Brindley High School

SENSES

(This is a poem about a part of my life from the past)

Sight
I see a rusty Skoda,
Sitting in the dim light,
Under a faint white lamp post,
It stood there very calm and still.

Sound
Clutter, clutter, the car goes along,
I hear a bang,
Smoke, black, ash, grey,
Nowhere to go,
I hear the rattling of the exhaust pipe,
The thumping of the engine,
Quiet whispers in the faint morning dew.

Taste
Bang goes the car,
Smoke everywhere,
The air is damp,
Tastes dim,
Tingling of the tongue,
Makes you feel all funny.

Smell
Smell the rustiness of the car,
The smell of smoke and fumes,
Faint but distinguished smells of oil,
Oil, colours, dim and unfoils.

Touch
Sharp peelings of rust,
Unfoiling from the car,
Dark colours in the light,
Of the faint white lamp post.

Joanne Skidmore (14)
Kingsbury School

THE VIEWING EXPERIENCE

One by one, like lambs to the slaughter,
Ushered along,
Hopeful, excited.

Into a room we are led,
Dim lights, dirty seats, tasteless music.

As we were settled, the lights dimmed out,
We began to whisper,
But we're met with a shout,
Quiet please, sit down!

Like demons descending from roof tops on high,
From above they came down with a screech and a cry,
Their torches ablaze with white fire and ice,
With voices that make even Arnie think twice,
Move forward please, don't throw popcorn.

The audience settled, a dark silence fell,
The curtain arose (although not too well),
The *Dolby* blew sound, the children blew raspberries,
The light from the screen threw wonder and magic.

Our brains were all ready, images flowed,
Ready to be brain-washed, make gaskets blown.

For two whole hours we'd sit there, alone,
Each in his world - then it's time to go home.

Ben Whitehead (14)
Kingsbury School

Venetian Backwaters

I stepped from the hustle and bustle of the milling crowds.
The boat gently rocked as I settled back into the red velvet.
With a swirl of the oar, the gondola slid from its berth.
The skilful gondolier weaved his way into the Venetian backwaters.

The voices of the crowds gave way to the echoes of the past -
The musty smell of decay and dereliction began to fill the air.
The water lapped softly against the shiny black paintwork,
Itself reflecting the misery of the Black Death.

I looked into the water's depths and caught a glimpse of a lady,
In black, on the balcony above. She held a mask to her face, but
Then the water rippled, I looked up but no-one was there.

Through the tranquility came the sound of a serenading gondolier,
His voice, strong and clear, resounded round the empty buildings.
Then further on we passed beneath the famous bridge -
The sighs of yesterday's condemned, replaced by the sighs of today's
Onlookers.

And so we emerged back into the hustle and bustle of the busy streets -
And back to reality.

Ian Thornhill (13)
Kingsbury School

For The Fun Of It

Getting lost around the town,
For the fun of it.
Late night discos; way too loud,
For the fun of it.

Ten minute walks to the beach,
For the fun of it.
Ice creams cost three pounds each,
For the fun of it.
Cleaning maids that wake you up,

For the fun of it.
Spanish chefs who can't cook,
For the fun of it.

Getting ready to go home,
For the fun of it.
The longest flight I've ever known,
    all for the fun of it.

Chris Field (13)
Kingsbury School

BONFIRE NIGHT

Fizz, bang, whoosh,
Fireworks glow in the sky.
All different colours,
making a spectacular sight.

Listen to the fire crackle and hiss,
as Guy Fawkes shrivels and dies.
Listen to the distant fireworks,
as they scream across the sky.

Smell baked potatoes,
being cooked round the fire.
Smell the fragrance
of sizzling marshmallows,
on their sticks.

Feel the sparklers,
as you run round the garden,
trying to write your name.

What a beautiful sight,
just hope it never ends.

Sarah Tonks (13)
Kingsbury School

THE WAR OF THE WAVES

The wind blows across the
sea to the shore
It batters the rocks
That stand like soldiers
To protect us all
The gulls like gliding bullets
fight the wind
The falling leaves like dying
people
The swaying trees like crumbly
houses
Then all is calm no gulls
no trees no leaves no wind
The waves are calm they
are like an all clear siren
The sun creeps out from its
shelter
The war is over.

Ria Mason (14)
Kingsbury School

INSPIRATION AND HOPE

When I looked at you, what did I see
All the things I wanted to be.
All those years of confrontations
Trying to meet your expectations

I was your puppet, you pulled my strings
Always striving for greater things
Now you're gone, how will I cope
You were my inspiration and hope

I tried to give you your satisfaction
To be your main attraction
How will I manage, now I'm free
To be the person I wanted to be

I think of all those happy years
The laughter that hides a million tears
I don't regret a thing I have done
Life with you was so much fun.

Kevin Kelly (13)
Kingsbury School

BANG

There was a smoky smell,
It reminded me of hell,
The fragrance lingered in the air,
As the fireworks burned away.

See the beautiful colours,
Hanging in the sky,
Some seem to fly.

I heard the anticipation
As the banger went off
the leaves behind me whistled
And then I was puzzled.

As I touched the sparkler,
My hands felt cold,
There was then a blur of gold.

There was a nice taste,
As it gave off a distinctive spice,
There was a unique spark as the air,
Was inhaled into our lungs.

Neil Beasley (13)
Kingsbury School

SWIMMING

Here lies the water waiting to swallow you,
In goes your foot,
Then the rest of your body,
You sink to the bottom,
But someone is always there to pull you up.

You gasp for air,
Panting for it,
Then you like it and love it,
You won't get out but in the end you have to,
You have no choice,
You get out, you start to get cold,
Then run to the changing room to get dry.

James Mortimer (13)
Kingsbury School

ALONE WITH MY THOUGHTS

They say there is a reason,
they say that time will heal,
but neither time nor reason
will change the way I feel.
No-one knows the heartache
that lies behind my smiles,
no-one knows how many times
I've broken down and cried,
I want to tell you something
so there won't be any doubt,
you're so wonderful to think of
so hard to live without.

Sarah Ellis (13)
Kingsbury School

Farm

I woke up early Friday morning
sheep bleating, horses neighing,
dogs barking, we were there at the farm.

Quick, quick get up, get out it's feeding
time for the lambs.
They skip, they jump, they dance about
now it's time for the cattle.

You put their food in that big long
trough with a bang, bang, crash.
They walk very slow then with a big gulp
the food is all now gone.

Push back you say to the horses with
a bucket of food in your hand you then
bang it on the manger and leave to
feed the dogs.

You walk in with a silver bowl and
put it on the floor, the dog comes and
eats it all, I say what a good boy you are.

Now it's time for my breakfast and I
wonder what I'll have, all I know
is that it won't be what they
have just had.

Amy Eaton (13)
Kingsbury School

OPERATION

Into the tall, dark, brown building,
Everywhere white beds, floors, walls,
With the lingering smell of disinfectant,
Smiling faces reassuring nods,
Take a seat someone said.
We waited, waited.
Time passing by it's getting closer,
Doors swinging shut with a clatter,
Squeaking trolley, being pushed by,
Telephone ringing,
Thank-you for calling.
I'm shown to a room
With a small white bed,
Told to be brave,
It will soon be over.
The doctor arrives notes in hand,
I'm put on a metal trolley,
Not long now
I'm feeling sleepy
I hear words with no meaning
Then silence the sleep.
Wake up Clare
It's all over now
My throat feels dry my eyes feel sore,
Back to sleep then the doctor arrives
Everything's fine you can go home soon.

Clare Marriott (13)
Kingsbury School

FIREWORKS

Up it shot like fiery flowers
waiting to explode then bang a
collection of colours came flurrying
down,
crimson, blue and gold.
It was the most beautiful
thing I'd ever seen.

Over to the barbecue I soon went
sausages were sizzling over the
rack, with all the excitement no-one
noticed they were crispy and black.
Toffee-apples to follow all sticky and
sweet,
no-one told me tonight would be such a
treat.

Holding the sparklers gave me a fright
as they dazzled and jumped showing
off their bright light.
Excitement took over as I wrote my
name and soon all the grown-ups
joined in my game.

When the night was all over and I
went to bed I could still hear
the noises buzzing in my head.
Whooshing, screeching, banging
Catherine wheels spinning and rockets whizzing.
What a wonderful night it had been!

Jennifer Bond (13)
Kingsbury School

THE SCREAM

A scream in the night
Not a thing in sight
A sound from down the hall, I heard a body fall
A bloody body on the floor
A sinister shadow, an open door.

A figure passes through the light, out the
Door and into the night
My face went cold
A chill of the spine
Then I heard the old clock chime,
The midnight hell had begun
I heard the time and then felt numb

I went back to the house to call for help,
'Hello, hello'
The line was dead.
Click, then I heard a gun to my head
He hit me hard in the leg followed it
up by a hit to the head.

He made his way out of sight
Deep into the very night. . .

Ian Davies (13)
Kingsbury School

BROKEN

As I leap high into the day sky,
As the world goes tumbling by,
As I hear the world fade, fade
Away into the distance.

As I scarcely plummet back down
To bumpy old ground,
The fear of realism comes floating back
Into my life,
As I hit the ground with a
Crash, crack, whack

Noise comes whispering back
As I fade, fade, fade, fade away.

Adam Cowell (14)
Kingsbury School

FUTURISTIC UNIVERSE

Here we are trapped on Earth,
Waiting for the space travel birth.
When will it come? Will it be soon?
Will my children be born on the Moon?

Maybe it will happen in the next ice age,
Then we can turn over a new history page.
Could we all invade the planets?
Or will our governments simply ban it?

Can't wait to be travelling up in the stars,
Drinking from the holographic bars.
Maybe I'll be living with friendly aliens.
Will we still be using paper and pens?

Katherine Wilcox (12)
Painsley R C High School

Lifeless Or Not?

The scrawled, grey pencil drawings lay on the page;
　　lifeless.
I lifted the paintbrush and poised it over the muscular
　　shoulder of the stallion,
As the moistened tip of the brush touched his body
　　the stallion seemed to shudder.
The smooth movement of the bristles across the page,
　　outlining the shapely contours of his quarters.
His head held high, his shining eyes gazing over the
　　deep valley below at his herd of excited foals
　　and graceful mares.
The foals leaping nimbly over the harsh rock outcrops
　　and chasing each other.
The sound of their neat hooves pounding on the unyielding
　　valley floor penetrating the still air,
Mares placidly observe their capers, breathing the cool
　　alpine air, fragrant with pine.
The sun sets behind the mountain ranges, shedding a
　　rainbow of colours onto the steep side of the
　　valley.
Reds, yellows, orange, the beautiful rainbow grows in
　　brightness, as the brush, its work now done,
　　returns to its tin.
The horses lie still on the page, no longer inanimate
　　but magnificent, filled with the vitality of life.

Hannah Mason (13)
Painsley R C High School

LIFE

You're stuck for 9 months in a squishy bag,
Then you're smothered when you're born,
By aunties, uncles, grandparents,
As time goes on the excitement wears off,
You are then taught to read, speak, write,
For the rest of your life you are told to shut up,
Then they send you to a prison, they call it school,
You spend the next 11 or 12 years there,
College, university, learning never ends,
While you are at school you become a teenager,
You undergo changes, mental and physical,
Relationships, arguments with parents,
problems, problems, problems,
As you grow older you need more and more things,
Clothes and shoes - fashion is a must.
The next thing you worry about is getting a job,
Clean hair, neat clothes, shiny shoes, punctuality,
Once you've got it, party, party, party,
The feeling is the worst in the world in the morning,
Then if you want to, you marry and have children,
More worries, money, bills to be paid, clothes for children,
Is there any point.
You get older, your children do the things you did,
Though in a different way,
You then become a grandparent, turn grey and draw pensions,
You begin to fear death,
But once you die there is nothing to fear,
You feel nothing,
And somewhere in the world, you have made room,
For new life to begin.

Kathryn Rushton (14)
Painsley R C High School

The Protester

'Ban the tests, ban the tests!'
Exclaim the angry crowd.
'Our fight never rests!'
They scream and shout aloud.

We head towards the dragon's lair,
I think of all my pets.
What if they were there?
At the hands of evil vets.

Suddenly a voice booms,
'Stay right away from me!'
Over me an ogre looms,
The crowd begin to flee.

I march through the lab door,
What a sight meets my eyes.
I see the looks of horror,
I hear the painful cries.

Animals locked in cages,
Cruelty through and through.
Why should animals suffer,
Because of humans, me and you?

Tested on for no reason,
Put through torture and pain.
Why is there vivisection?
Because some people are vain.

I advance towards the first cage,
When I feel my arm being jerked.
I turn around in horror and rage,
Behind me the enemy lurked.

In sadness I walk away,
Filled with remorse and sorrow.
I couldn't save them today,
But I've still got tomorrow.

Kerry Lockett (13)
Painsley R C High School

YORKSHIRE

The majestic mountains dominated the horizon,
enshrouded by a cloak of mist.
The sky was dull, the day threatening
moisture was the scent in the air.

A lonely farmer on an outcrop of rock,
humidity seeping through his clothes,
sheep huddled together for warmth
and the cold penetrated everywhere.

The mist invaded each dry corner
blanketing familiar landscape
the cold rough grey stone of the castle
an outpost of medieval life.

Yorkshire's given us its worst elements
now the sun breaks the barrier of cloud
the valleys bathed in golden light,
and life continues as before.

Clare Parry (14)
Painsley R C High School

MODERN TECHNOLOGY

As technology increases rapidly,
we leave the century of improvement,
and enter a new age,
an age in which we will live forever.
Technology and industry are becoming more lethal,
we have the ability to obliterate earth.

Computers are improving all the time,
soon they will be able to store information automatically,
they will almost become human brains.
If computers become too powerful,
we might be endangered,
soon they will control life and death.

Industry is expanding all the time,
soon we will only live in cities,
there will be no country or forests.
If we are not careful, pollution will ruin the earth,
we will have to live in oxygenated domes,
away from all of the pollution outside.

I can't wait for the time when cars will fly,
the time when you will be able to travel the speed of light,
to reach your destination before you depart,
the time when you can teleport from one place to another,
the time when you can travel to distant galaxies,
and even discover a parallel universe.

War is a major subject nowadays,
if there was a World War III it would only last 10 minutes,
the whole world would become a floating atomic mass,
the complete inhabitance of the earth would become extinct.
Nuclear bombs are the most formidable weapon,
the world and the people are not safe.

Anthony Gamble (14)
Painsley R C High School

HOME

Home is just an old building,
Where a group or family may be,
Where one may keep assets and belongings,
Home isn't much to me.

Home is a place one feels calm in,
A house one can call an abode.
A place where one can come back to,
A place you can just call your own.

Home is a place you can live in,
With a floor, a roof and some walls,
A pile of bricks with cement in.
A house, not a home anymore.

Home is a place you can rest in,
With family relations and friends.
Home is a place where one feels one is wanted,
Home is where love never ends.

Home is a house full of objects,
A chore that's a pain to keep clean.
A place where one eats and one sleeps in.
That's all, for me, that it means.

Home isn't just an old building
Where a group or a family may be.
Be it castle, palace or cavern,
Home is everything to me.

Alex Durling (14)
Painsley R C High School

The Highland Mist

High up, on a pinnacle, in the bleak silence of the highlands,
where only the utterances of the wind gather to chant their phantom
like a chorus is a view,
not seen by many and treasured by few.

The renewed freshness of the autumn morning
awakens the wildlife of the hill,
from their dormant state within their habitations on the heights
of the moors.

The virginally settled dew glistens upon the brilliant
fresh grass,
the sun has managed to pierce the cloak of mist surrounding
everything upon blatant peaks.

From the great heights, looking down into the deep majestic
valleys,
there is a blanket of mist which shrouds all below it,
except for a few tall emergent trees that have escaped
the clutches of the mist.

Owen Griffiths (13
Painsley R C High School

Teenage Years

Teenage years must be the worst
all parents do is swear and curse
You do nothing right, everything wrong
don't despair, leave home before long.

You fall in love or so to speak
your handsome prince, your knees go weak
he walks your way or so you think
his eyes meet hers, hearts just sink.

Forget about men, at least you try,
a girls' night out, have a good cry.
Watch a movie, have some fun
forget about men and what they've done.

I'll do my best, to stay alive
a few more years, I hope to survive
I hope to manage these next few
years,
as teenage years must be the worst.

Jennifer Temple-Smith (14)
Painsley R C High School

WHO CAN? HOW CAN?

Unbelief, disbelief, does anyone really know,
Who Santa is, or why he is, and do we need to know?
Everyone needs something, that isn't really real,
To think about, to hide behind, to conceal how we feel.
Inside each of us is Santa, jolly, kind and good,
Loving, caring, sharing, if I could, I really would,
Be like that each and every day, but it is difficult to be,
As honest, real and gentle, as Santa is to me.

Charles Okell (14)
Painsley R C High School

MY DREAM ABOUT YOU!

Everything around was quiet, tranquil.
The wind was softly blowing but all else was still.
You and me together, sitting side by side.
Watching the sunset over the sea,
the gentle sway of the tide.
It all seemed so wonderful,
I wished it would never end.
You're the one on which I depend.
We sat around the fire you made, looking at our star.
I'd never felt so close to you, you were near but never far.
It was now really dark so we decided to walk.
As we strolled along the sands, you began to talk.
You told me that you loved me and would never leave my side,
At first I didn't believe you, but you never lied.
We'd been together for so long, but never did I view.
The scene that would end our happy lives.
We'd still be together in our place near the flowing tides.
But that never happened, we had eternal life.
That was my dream the night before I became your wife.

Laura Smith (15)
Painsley R C High School

THE TIGER

The powerful tiger shadows its prey in the long,
    brown grass.
The mysterious eyes fix upon the unfortunate animal.
The tiger creeps forward, silently approaching its
    prey.
The deer senses something in the grass, it looks round,
But too late, the mighty tiger crouches, then
    pounces on the panic stricken animal.
When the dust settles, the tiger and the deer
    have vanished,
Leaving only footprints in the dust.

The tiger's way of life is being destroyed
    by deforestation, by medicine, by man.
The tiger is a victim of the industrial revolution.
Man is trying to become the king of kings in
    the animal world,
They have to make space for themselves.
They make space by killing animals.
The animals of today may not be the animals of
    tomorrow.
            Killed, by man.

Stewart Fisher (13)
Painsley R C High School

THE AMUSEMENT PARK
(A word to funfair lovers)

Let's all go to the funfair.
The big wheel's incredibly quick,
Let's all go to the funfair,
'Please mum, I think Timmy's been sick'

For remember, folks, at the funfair
You get spun around and around.
You get off and think you're so cool.
(That's before you collapse on the ground)

You go surging down the log flume,
Over a 100 ft drop.
As you get to the bottom and realise
Your stomach's been left at the top.

You wriggle yourself into the seat,
For the new Jurassic Park ride,
And you're suddenly seized by a terrible urge
To leap out, and run, and hide.

The meat pies are incredibly suspect,
Cos they don't contain any meat,
Instead they're constructed from pure BSE
And smell just like Grandmother's feet.

You emerge bruised and battered,
With a horrible urge to spew,
But it's a British institution,
Oh, I love the funfair, don't you?

Andrew Walton (12)
Painsley R C High School

BONFIRE NIGHT

Flames arise from all around me
Sparkles, twinkles and golden sparks.

Fireworks flood the sky with colour
the darkness is tinted with radiant stripes

A guy is erected, haggard and bent
Flames licking up at its tattered rags.

Smells drift over from the gigantic bar-b-que
Mingling with the clouds of grey-white smoke.

People are milling all around me
Shouting, singing, chatting and playing

Children's faces are a glowing crimson
Steam puffing out of their gaping mouths

The hot dogs are served, there begins a mad rush.
the little ones push to the front of the line

Bottles are corked, wine is poured
Glasses tinkle as a toast is made

The tower of flames die down to embers
The air around is a stifling heat.

A wave of rockets go up with a scream
Catherine wheels whiz to everyone's delight

The clock strikes 12, the guests disperse
The fun is over, the fireworks spent

I arrive home and climb into bed
I dream of all the enjoyment I saw tonight.

Thomas Dougherty (13)
Painsley R C High School

THE SACK

Sitting by the factory wall
The wall so big and I so small
I hear machines, whirring within
What did I do? What was my sin?
What will my mother say? What will my father say?
Will they be angry? Will they send me far away?
Will I get another job? What will it be?
Will I go to London? What will I see?
Will I see poverty? Will I see wealth?
Will I see sickness? Will I see health?
Whatever I am and whatever I'll be
You'll always be you and I'll always be me.

Kathryn Hopkins (12)
Painsley R C High School

THE BEDROOM

The smell was amazing, the carpet no more,
Piles of old clothes were blocking the door.
Half eaten homework was the hamster's new nest
He tried last week's socks but found this was best.
The cupboard was open and through the crack you could see,
A family of mice enjoying yesterday's tea.
The girl could recite the mother's words in her head,
'This litter's disgusting and just look at the bed.'
The core of an apple was next to the bin,
The door then creaked open as the mother walked in.
At the sight of the room she fell by the door,
'Mother,' said daughter, 'Don't litter the floor!'

Emma Cooke (12)
Painsley R C High School

ANTARCTICA

Far far away in the icy south
Floated a Weddell seal near a glacier mouth.
The icy waters of the southern flow
Warmer yet than where blizzards blow
Now dark both night and day.
He's waiting for a penguin to swim his way.
Up above where the eggs are warm
Comes a terrible whirring from a shapeless form.
Helicopters! The eggs deserted become the skua's feast.
The Adelies are uneasy to say the least
Food forgotten the seal calls out.
Other danger lurks there is no doubt.
Cracking, crushing pushing through the ice
Man-made monsters don't know the price
That wild ancient world will have to pay
Why oh why won't you go away.

Katie May (12)
Painsley R C High School

THE CRUELTY OF MAN

Watch out here comes another one, timber,
the thought of the tree loggers makes
me shiver.
The terrible squeal of the chainsaw,
against wood with memories of the first war,
The regular call of timber echoes around
the forest,
as the newly born macaw is felled from
a nest.

James Lander (13)
Painsley R C High School

ENDANGERED SPECIES

Monkeys are endangered,
They soon could all be dead,
I think about this dreadful thought,
While lying in my bed.

They really are so harmless,
They can't hurt you at all,
People shoot them in a tree,
Then to the ground they fall.

There are many endangered species,
All dying in the wild,
Why don't you help them,
It'll please a little child.

It only costs a small amount,
It doesn't cost a lot,
Please help them and sponsor one,
Forever - these animals are not.

Jo Alcock (12)
Painsley R C High School

THE DRUG ADDICT

Through visions of blur and darkness,
With new beauty, new sound and new colour.
The addict sees the world before him,
And as it lasts he lives in hope.

The journeys through colour and sound,
Get shorter and shorter each time.
As he experiences the travel through time,
His life gets shorter and shorter.

As the price is hard to pay,
He gets it cheap from the dealer.
Everytime he comes back to earth,
The world gets darker and darker.

Through visions of blur and darkness,
As he experiences the travel through time.
His life gets shorter and shorter,
It's the thrill that keeps him alive.

Charlotte Hurst (12)
Painsley R C High School

HALLOWE'EN

That night the moon was full
There was magic in the air
Peace had been and gone
As the witches left their lair.

That night there was no rest
the stars had an eerie glow
Chants, charms and spells were shrieked and screamed
As the seeds of Black Magic were sown.

That night all evil had broken forth
The reign of good was at an end
The winds blew round and lightning flashed
As the curses of witches were sent.

That night was long and held much fright
that night was full of fear
But evil rules never more
For another year . . .

Rebecca Brentnall (13)
Painsley R C High School

Is This What It Was For?

The carnage of the battle,
The mangled vehicles plastered in blood,
Bodies, legs and arms apart,
The dead and dying in the mud.

Nuclear warheads, tanks and planes,
Crashed and burning in the sand,
Ammunition, guns and mines,
Silence rules, where soldiers used to stand.

The stink of rotten bodies,
the smell drifting in the air,
Nothing to hear, nothing at all,
The taste of dust, defeat and despair.

The madness of this fighting,
the mourning for the dead,
What is the point - Is there one?
Peace lies just ahead.

Troop movements were the reason,
Two countries fought a war,
A continent ripped apart,
Is this what it was for?

Gavin Stephens (13)
Painsley R C High School

Sea Shore

The waves tossed away the rocks from the cliffs,
The sea spray tremendous, it was just as if,
We had picked it ourselves, even hand picked the shells.
Everything perfect, everything right,
Beautiful by day, beautiful by night.

A ship pulled in the harbour, and gave a loud call,
As if it were to say, I'm coming through all.
As a seagull flew over, an ice-cream van drove by,
The ice-cream so white looked like the clouds from the sky.
the sky was so blue, the clouds were so white,
Beautiful by day, beautiful by night.

As your feet sink in the sand, your bucket in hand,
Sun cream on your face, a towel round your waist.
As you look to the sky, a kite flies by,
Such a wonderful height,
Beautiful by day, beautiful by night.

A sandcastle washed away by the tide,
The sunset so brilliant, the horizon so wide.
As you head away home, away from the beach,
You look at your skin, a warm colour peach.
The day is now going, it's close drawing night,
Beautiful by day, beautiful by night.

Rachel Ayres (12)
Painsley R C High School

IMAGINE

Imagine the giant elephants
With their trunks raised in the air
A bullet shot into their side
And the hunter doesn't care.

Imagine the great whale
With its head caught in a net
And a harpoon sticking in its side
Yet still it's not quite dead.

Imagine the playful seal
Lying without a coat
On the cold hard snow of the Arctic
The killer stands to gloat.

Imagine the patterned tiger
With a blank look on his face
A tranquilliser shot from afar
To wipe out the endangered race.

Imagine the Chinese panda
Sprawled out in all the bamboo
Killed to make some medicine
The beneficiary of course is you

These animals are in danger
They're dying day by day
We need to do something about it
If we want them all to stay

If this poem makes you sad
Or even makes you cry
Then take one moment to think
And ask yourself why?

Sarah Mason (13)
Painsley R C High School

THEME PARK

Out of the car and onto the train
Off we go to the theme park again

A buzz of excitement builds in the queue
As one by one we're let through

Aim for the ride you think best
Get to the front before the rest

Heartbeat thumping
Adrenaline pumping

Shrieks of laughter fill the air
As we fly round the track with the wind in our hair

On to the next one, strap yourself in
Faster and faster, we start to spin

Delighted children shout and scream
Whirling and twirling in a dream

Heartbeat pacing
Adrenaline racing

It's time for the flume, so in we get
I hope this time we don't get wet

But down the chute, I'm covered with spray
Never mind - it's the end of the day

Out through the gates and onto the train
To take us back to the car again

Back home now, dry, warm and weary
A day at the theme park can never be dreary

Heartbeat slowing
Adrenaline - Gone!

Kirsty Hill (12)
Painsley R C High School

WHEN I GROW UP

When I grow older what will I do
Will I be a teacher or work in a zoo?
Maybe I won't have a job afterall
Maybe I'll work in a market stall.

When I get older who will I marry
Maybe I'll be the next Mrs Larry
I might even have a child or two
And if I'm lucky I'll have a pet too.

When I get older will I have money
Will every day of my life be sunny?
Will I be a millionaire or very poor
Will I have money or could there be room for more ?

When I get older, what will I be like
Will I sit around all day or walk and take hikes?
When I get older will I have good health
Where will I live - in the north or the south?

When I get older will I become blind
Maybe I'll start to lose my mind
Will I still be able to walk
Maybe I won't even hear people talk.

Lisa Emery (12)
Painsley R C High School

AT THE SEASIDE

Seagulls everywhere I look,
Dad's sitting and reading a book.

My little brother is playing in the sand,
Grandmas and Grandads listening to the band.

Tourists shopping all around,
Children at the beach-side fairground.

Oh no the sea is coming in,
Children screaming and making a din.

The beach is empty everyone has gone home,
There are just a few people having a roam.

Craig Chappell (12)
Painsley R C High School

DRIFTER

Drifting right out here,
From earth you cannot see,
Mercury, Venus, Mars,
Other planets and galaxies.

Drifting round in orbit,
Meteors shooting by,
Balls of gas and fire,
Dancing by and by.

There goes a shooting star,
Make a wish and quick,
Before it burns out.
You'll miss it if you blink.

Moons floating round planets,
Like dots in the empty place.
Look into the emptiness,
Look right up into space.

Dominic McDonnell (12)
Painsley R C High School

THE BERLIN WALL/BORDER OF DOOM

When I went to visit my sister,
I did not expect that when I returned,
The huge, cold, solid, chunk of concrete
Would prevent me from reaching home.
Nobody's sure who built it
No-one will admit.
It was clear in the morning and the next day, on
The darker side of the wall, people ran into it not
Expecting the border of doom.

I never saw my sister until 1989 when the
Colourful, graffited slabs of brick were knocked
Down by the Republic of People who wanted to meet
Their relations they had left on the other side.
Pieces have been sold to remember the pain and
Sorrow of wondering if your mother has passed
Away or your house is still standing.
Nothing could compensate for the anger and
Emotion.
No other piece of stone has ever brought more
News and unity than the Border of Doom.

Julia Lund (13)
Painsley R C High School

THE HUNTER

Bang!
A gunshot rings through the air
What's the hunter got this time?
A rabbit, a hare?

As ruby red blood
Trickles from its side
The hunter is feeling
A sense of pride.

As through tears,
My vision fades
I think of the price
This animal has paid.

And I don't think it's fair
And that's simply because,
If animals were humans,
Would they shoot down us?

Alexandra Somerfield (12)
Polesworth High School

ONLY A MEMORY

You write as you sit beside me,
Your hand moves the pen,
And I stare at the hand,
Dreaming of things that we could do.
You look up,
I smile,
You smile back.
We gaze at each other,
I stare into your pale blue eyes,
What are you thinking?
What do you see?
The moment is perfect and I feel great.
Then, the pen moves and you look away,
The moment is gone,
Then you are too.
I sit alone in the room,
The light is dim,
My pen stops moving,
Time to think, time to remember,
But why must I only have memories when I want you?

Nathan Askew (15)
Polesworth High School

First Born

First born, and heir to the family pride,
Neither of us could escape your shadow,
As a child, I could not find a flaw in your genius,
Though I tried.

For your parents, your chosen subject was
territory unknown,
While you were here, I listened, looked, learned
When you were not, your technology stood
alone.

I lost interest, because I knew it was useless
to try and emulate you,
Though you were a mystery to me,
While others had doubts about you,
I just knew.

You stood in the light, whilst I stood in
the dark,
But looking into your beam was enlightenment
enough,
I always fell, but you cushioned my fall,
You were always stronger when things got
rough.

When I got older you became one of us,
We were like one another,
I saw you make mistakes and although
no longer a genius,
You became a brother.

Helen Birkinshaw (16)
Polesworth High School

THE HEALER

I watched through
eyes of salty tears,
the woman who always
took away my worst fears.

She gently wiped away
the tears with a smile,
a special one - beautiful,
in its own particular style.

She unwound the bandage,
and bound up my knee,
then fastened with a pin,
I watched anxiously.

Her gentle fingers,
with perfect nails,
a steady hand
that never fails.

She stabbed at the
cotton wool, with TCP,
and her worried expression
sympathised with me.

Now I don't cry over
a little cut knee,
I cry over things
that she just cannot see.

Rebecca Byrne (15)
Polesworth High School

THE POLAR BEAR

Slipping, sliding down the icy mountain,
It's cold but I am bold.
Facing the harshness of the wind,
Stumble, tumble my fur is covered in snow.
A familiar figure approaches and,
As we glide together downwards,
We meet other bears.
Large and small all join in the fun.
It's time to go when the sun goes in,
So we sleepily climb the icy mountain.

Robyn Catley (12)
Queen Elizabeth's Mercian School

TIGER TIGER

Tiger Tiger in your cage
What's it like to be locked up?
Not free to roam around
But living off their ends of meat.

Tiger Tiger in your cage
What's it like to be locked up?
I just hate, it can I go
To be free with all my friends.

Tiger Tiger in your cage
What's it like to be locked up?
Just like a slave who's done nothing wrong
Please can I be free like you?

I'm not just a puppet show on display
So do something about it before I'm gone.

Anastasia Cassie (11)
Queen Elizabeth's Mercian School

BUSY BUSY BUMBLE BEES

Busy busy bumble bees
Collecting pollen on their knees,
Busy busy bumble bees
Making honey for men to make money,
Busy busy bumble bees
Always flying around the trees,
Busy busy bumble bees
You know they never sneeze,
Busy busy bumble bees.

Sammy England (11)
Queen Elizabeth's Mercian School

DOLPHIN

Why don't we go for a ride on a dolphin,
Splashing around the sea,
We'll visit his mum,
We'll have lots of fun,
We might even stay for our tea.
So why don't we go for a ride on a dolphin.

Katie Gilmour (11)
Queen Elizabeth's Mercian School

THE RED SQUIRREL

Leaping from tree to tree,
Rusty red flashing as he bounds,
His bushy tail curving to swing from branch to branch,
He pricks his ears as a nut catches his sight,
Now, grasping the nut in his paws, he nibbles,
His blackberry eyes gleaming,
He's off again bounding out of sight.

Siân Jones (11)
Queen Elizabeth's Mercian School

ELEPHANT

Elephants so big and round.
Little of them left.
People kill them.
Hey, leave them alone.
Elephants why are you killing them?
All of them, no just most of them.
Nothing's important about them.
Too many are dying. *Stop.*

Leigh-Anne Barrett (11)
Queen Elizabeth's Mercian School

WALKING IN THE JUNGLE

Walking in the jungle
Looking here and there
A big pair of eyes,
looking with a glare,
Is it a tiger?
Is it a bear?
Is it a lion with a long mop of hair?
Looking around,
what do I see?
Monkeys swinging from tree to tree,
Down below,
It's dark and dim,
What will I see next,
I think with a grin,
In the distance,
I can see,
Buffaloes oxen and an ape staring at me.

David Moore (11)
Queen Elizabeth's Mercian School

PUSSY

Pussy can sit by the fire and sing,
Pussy can climb a tree,
Or play with a silly old string
To amuse herself not me.

Tom Warrier (11)
Queen Elizabeth's Mercian School

TIGERS

Female tigers prowling,
Male tigers growling.
Going through the grass,
In a great mass.

Walking, walking, walking,
Going really slow,
Getting faster and faster,
Like the speed of light,
Running through the grass in the night.

He slows down walking, walking, walking,
Still going slow.
Now he goes home,
Chewing a bone,
He goes to sleep,
Without a peep.

Dean Sale (12)
Queen Elizabeth's Mercian School

THE PANDA

The panda is black and white,
And is scared with fright,
He wanders and wanders,
Into a lonely jungle,
And never finds his way,

The panda has big brown eyes,
He lies and lies and lies,
You see the panda is lazy,
And someday will go crazy,
But never cries as he tries.

Laura Brookes (12)
Queen Elizabeth's Mercian School

ASIAN TIGER

Lush and green and far away
Getting smaller every day.
A home for animals great and small
A home for the greatest of them all.

Asian forest steaming hot
Reduced in size man's devious plot.
Watched so closely by amber eyes
Another tree is cut and dies.

The tiger's numbers will be none
When the trees have almost gone.
Stripy orange, black and white
Moving slowly by starlight.

An Asian forest shrinking fast
Tigers always would come last.
Man is poaching food and home
The tiger has nowhere to roam.

Are we to let this crime go by
Should we let the tiger die.
Should to help be our endeavour
Extinction really means forever.

Ben Robinson (11)
Queen Elizabeth's Mercian School

THE ORCA

The Orca glides slowly through the sea,
Jumping and swimming happily.

Beautiful creatures, this is true,
What do other people think, how about you?

Kill them, cut them they're all gone,
Extinct forever, is this what we want?

Save this creature before it's too late,
Facing extinction is this their fate?

So if you want this creature true,
You'd better think of something to do.

Melanie Veal (12)
Queen Elizabeth's Mercian School

PANDAS IN DANGER

The panda is in danger,
They're getting less and less,
Do yourself a favour,
And give your gun a rest.

Pandas are big and soft,
Pandas are black and white,
They walk around on all fours,
And go to sleep at night.

Please stop killing the pandas,
It's not like you at all,
You can roll them like a ball,
You must be really cruel.

Sarah Ashwood (13)
Queen Elizabeth's Mercian School

ELEPHANTS

I love animals and they love me
All of these who die I cry
They are lovely to cuddle
With their big trunks and their big feet
Elephants are the ones for me.

Aaron Watterson (12)
Queen Elizabeth's Mercian School

CRICKET

As I come into bat in the middle order,
A lot of things go through my head.
Will I score any runs?
Will the next ball be dead?
Will I last the rest of this over?
Will I be out first ball?
I'm ready for the first delivery,
Thank God! It's a no-ball

Second ball, third ball, fourth and fifth,
Ready to face the sixth.
Thank God! At last! I'm off the mark,
Off the mark with a six!

All the way through the innings I go,
I'm on seventy-two not-out.
My partner is the last man
Doh! He's lobbed the ball and is caught out!

My highest score ever
Is seventy-two
I'm not even a batsman, either
And it's only my debut.

Dan Vallance (13)
Queen Elizabeth's Mercian School

Euro '96

3 o'clock the game kicks off,
The teams are England and Spain,
From the crowd not a blink not a cough,
England will win the competition.

Gazza looks good,
But Manjinj looks better,
Spain look promising,
But England are better.

England go in,
Venables unhappy,
As old tactics are thrown in the bin,
Two goals have been scored but also disallowed.

The referees whistle blows,
It's penalties all around,
England are chosen to take first,
But from the crowd not a single sound.

Shearer scores first,
The second goes to Platt,
The crowd are going to burst,
Come on England do us proud.

England win,
Thanks to Seaman saving the day,
England in excitement,
As Spain's manager has a lot to say.

Steven Deakin (13)
Queen Elizabeth's Mercian School

THE WORLD OUR HOME

The world is our home
Yet so many people are alone
So many people crying
So many people dying
The world is so small
But rises up tall
With animals fighting and
Bolts of lightning
Humans invading
Saying the land is theirs
Marching on in threes and pairs
To see people so selfish and cruel
To see no-one helping even if they rule
It makes you think it was a big mistake
To destroy a world which God has given
To kill people because of their colour or race
To kill them so there isn't any trace
It's not right to kill and fight
It's not right to destroy and burn
Let's change let's make a turn
To start a new
For me and you
Let's not face it alone
Let's join together and
Make it our home forever.

Vanessa Higgins (13)
Queen Elizabeth's Mercian School

THE TRAGEDY AT DUNBLANE

Eleven o'clock,
It was an enormous shock,
Sixteen children and teacher died,
At Dunblane primary school.

The young children
Were having fun,
Until a man entered
The gymnasium, with a gun.

He killed sixteen children
And their teacher too,
There was no warning,
It came out of the blue.

They were scared and innocent,
Their parents shed tears,
A silence was held,
By all their peers.

Tom was his name,
He killed himself - *was he insane?*
After all, he was the one to blame,
For the horrific killing, at Dunblane.

Rebecca Jones (13)
Queen Elizabeth's Mercian School

THE TIGER

The tiger is a hunter,
It searches for its food,
Looking high and looking low,
Waiting for his food.

Running into major trouble,
People he can see,
A gun shot takes him down and down,
He's now hanging from a tree.

Bye bye tiger people say,
As they make sure he gets on his way.

Lee Marsh (12)
Queen Elizabeth's Mercian School

BEARS

Bears are big and look scary,
But bears are in danger,
People shoot and destroy their homes,
Only to sell them at an outrageous price,

Bears in a circus,
Bears wearing chains,
Bears bearing blisters,
Dancing in pain,
Bears begging for food,
Only to die in the grotty zoos.

Zara Curley (12)
Queen Elizabeth's Mercian School

PLANET MORGAN

Nobody knew,
It was so shocking,
The smell was putrid,
Repulsive, disgraceful, vile.

Staring in the darkness,
Illuminated by its neighbour the sun,
Glistening flashes, an airy sparkle,
Blinding flares with blinding glow,
Vivid gaudy lights.

The colossal rotating planet,
Immense, gigantic, mighty spinning on an invisible pole,
Dwarfing its moon,
With a turquoise veil hiding its hidden features.

Harsh landscape,
Scattered with boulders and cobbled rocks,
Hoarse gruff, rasping noise as bubbles of toxic gases
erupt through the
turbulent lava.

Samantha Clements (13)
Queen Elizabeth's Mercian School

THE HUNTER

Man of the plains,
Run at speed,
Wind through your name.
See your prey -
Stalk it first.
Could this be your meals for all of today?
Keep low, sneak through,
Careful - it might see you!
Gliding silently, so graceful.
Could your life ever be dull?

There it goes, just a flick of the head,
It's set off now,
It knows it'll soon be dead.
It's running for its life,
Just a second too late!
Your claws stick in like a knife.
There you are - your catch of the day.
You give a squeal of pride,
You've caught your prey!

Laura Dolphin (12)
Queen Elizabeth's Mercian School

THE DOLPHIN

Watch them jump
Watch them fall
Watch them catch a bouncing ball
People kill them for silly things
Like their fins.

Are you one of those people
Catching them in nets
Taking away their freedom
Just like caged-up pets.

They are living animals
They don't deserve to die
They should roam around the waters
And jump up to the sky.

Natalie Parboo (12)
Queen Elizabeth's Mercian School

THE ELEPHANT

Here comes the elephant swaying along,
His legs are in leather,
And padded his toes,
He can root up an oak,
With a whisk of his nose,
With a wave of his trunk,
And a turn of his chin,
He can pull down a house,
Or pick up a pin,
Beneath his grey forehead,
A little eye peers,
Or what is he thinking,
Between those wide ears?
What does he feel?

But that grey forehead,
Those crinkled ears,
Have learned to be kind in a hundred years.

There goes the tusks to be sold at an auction
The elephants are at caution,
Their ivory is worth loads,
All to build new roads.

Kerry Cross (12)
Queen Elizabeth's Mercian School

THE GREAT WHITE SHARK

I swoop down, down below,
Deeper and deeper I will go,
Quick there's a fish,
I want it on my dish.

I circle it with curiosity,
I could bite it with ferocity,
No it's too small and thin,
Onward searching I must swim.

Wow! What's that meal;
It looks like a seal,
I have a bite,
It kicks with fright.

Err it's a mesh!
It tastes like flesh,
It's no good,
I'm covered in blood.

Suddenly I hear a shot of a gun,
The last thing I see is the glimpse of the sun,
I was the master of the sea in which I reign,
Until man imposed himself into my domain.

Carl Green (13)
Queen Elizabeth's Mercian School

POOR RHINO

Poor Rhino standing all forlorn,
They only want you for your horn,
Your leathered skin baked in the sun,
Is no protection from a gun.

You tried your best, you gave your all,
But one loud bang and there you fall,
They take your horn that's all they need,
A carcass left where others feed.

Against a gun you can't fight back,
Death for Aphrodisiac

Louise Griffiths (12)
Queen Elizabeth's Mercian School

THE BLACK PANTHER

The black panther sleeps in the trees,
He has a glistening black coat and charcoal eyes,
He paces after his prey,
The panther leaps onto the victim's back,
He sinks his teeth and rips his flesh,
Streak of blood left behind,
Deep in the long grass man hunts his target,
Ready aim *fire,*
The panther falls to the floor in pain, lifeless.

Gareth Lewis (12)
Queen Elizabeth's Mercian School

THE TIGER

The tiger is a beautiful creature that lives in the grass,
It lies in wait for a meal to pass.

Then the bang of a gun,
Surely killing innocent creatures is no fun.

Its bones are in medicine,
Its skin is in rugs,
All this is done by some horrible thugs.

The tiger is dying the tiger is dying,
The tiger is crying.

Graeme May (12)
Queen Elizabeth's Mercian School

DOLPHIN DANGER

The dolphins splashing through
the waves.
In and out of the rocky caves,
The dolphins go swimming all
through the days,
Jumping together through the
rippling waves.
He and his friend's beautiful tale
But if we don't watch it and
stop all the torture.
They will be forgotten tales.
Danger, danger, danger, danger!

Natalie Moran (12)
Queen Elizabeth's Mercian School

PANDA

It's black and white,
Fat and nice,
It looks cuddly and is as furry as can be.
It chews on bamboo.
Its eyes are wide it looks so sad.
That it has to go in a zoo to keep from being shot.
It longs to roam free but it never can.

Rebecca O'Brien (12)
Queen Elizabeth's Mercian School

SAVE THE WHALES

Happily swimming in the sea
Jumping up and down up and down.
Then a sharp pain!
Oh the pain!
It's that huge thing - a harpoon gun.
They wind you leaving a trail of blood,
Crash! And a bit more pain,
Poor soul he hit the ship,
Slowly . . . slowly . . . slowly . . . Dead.

Joanne Parnham (12)
Queen Elizabeth's Mercian School

FISHES!

Have you ever thought about fishes,
Being caught day after day,
Being killed for pleasure,
To think of them becoming extinct.

Just think, hooks caught in lips,
Pain just for food,
Is it really any pleasure?
Is it really any leisure?

I never thought of fish being endangered,
But now I think we should do something,
How about holding a protest?
Or maybe should we lay back and have a rest?

Adam Roberts (12)
Queen Elizabeth's Mercian School

EXTINCT

Extinct isn't a very big word yet it's all over
The world
The food chain is being broken one by one for
Food and fur and a bit of fun.
A tiger is used from head to claw,
Yet the reason for doing it is very poor.
What gives us the right to stop an animal give
Birth - believe it or not it's not just our earth.
All the animals' trees are being cut down into
horrible stubble ground.
Soon there will be no animals around just so
we can earn an extra few pounds!

Hannah Bridges (12)
Queen Elizabeth's Mercian School

TIGER BEHIND BARS

The tiger has enemies, fears, and fate,
But keep all his feelings locked up in his cage,
Where that cruel one - man
Put him there on a stage.
He walks back and forth -
Pacing up,
Pacing down.
People are staring, but what's there to see?
A poor helpless creature, longing to be free?
He was taken from his home,
He was happy out there.
But he can't do a thing -
It just is not fair.
He started as many,
But now he is few.
Because man is destroying his place in the wild.
Don't kill them for fun, just because it's the style.
Tigers have rights,
As do human beings.
So stop all this cruelty,
And help them to thrive,
We want to as well,
So let's keep them alive.

Ceri Summers (12)
Queen Elizabeth's Mercian School

WHALE KILLER

Along comes the whaler in his ship,
Sailing as the waves curl and rip.
Sailing home to see his wife,
Ending another hump whale's life.
The whales do us no harm,
Their beautiful makings only charm.
Jumping out of the snarly sea,
Free as free can ever be,
Until the fisherman with his harpoon gun,
Ends a life before it has begun.
Leave these graceful creatures be,
They deserve only to be free.

Nicola Watkins (13)
Queen Elizabeth's Mercian School

ELEPHANT

Elephants, elephants,
And their funny trunks,
Why do people hunt,
For their tusks,
Maybe they are worth money,
But they don't get funny,
The beautiful colour of their dark eyes,
And the weight of their huge feet,
Elephants could kill you,
But really they are harmless,
So why all this hunting,
They are no harm to you,
It's not fair,
Why let them suffer too.

Laura Wiggall (13)
Queen Elizabeth's Mercian School

THE TIGER

There was a little tiger,
Who went out to play,
He didn't know what was out there,
But he wasn't going to stay.

Behind the tree was it,
The thing was lurking there,
He was going to catch the tiger in a pit,
And didn't really care,

There was a gunshot in the air,
The tiger ran like mad,
The tiger thought it's not fair,
And it's very bad.

Suzanne Whitmore (13)
Queen Elizabeth's Mercian School

ANIMALS OF THE WILD SIDE

Think of the wild side,
  Where's the king of the jungle,
    The fast moving tiger,
      And the happy swinging monkey.
        Happiness was once bought here,
          But now is just a place of sadness,
            'cause of the horrible humans,
              locking them in cages, kept as pets
                And make money out of them.
                  When will this place return to happiness
                    And joy as it was before?
                      Someday it shall be done!

Sin Yee Wong (12)
Queen Elizabeth's Mercian School

DREAM

I dreamt I saw you,
Standing in a Pacific Sunset,
Laughing, smiling and melting my heart.
I dreamt of you,
Dreaming of me
Dreaming of you.
Loving you.
Always loving you.
Eternally.

Samantha Kennett (11)
Rising Brook High School

MUM

Through all of the sadness
Through all of the tears
You were strong for us
You didn't share your fears

Through all of the grief
Through all of the pain
You've tried for us
Often in vain

We don't seem to notice
We don't seem to care
But our world would collapse
If you were not there.

No matter what happens
You will pull us through
But even if you couldn't
We won't stop loving you.

Geraldine Bradley (16)
Rising Brook High School

MY LIFE AS A HORSE

Today is Sunday my day of rest,
This is the day that I like best,
Galloping free my mane in the air.
Prancing and trotting without a care.

I work at the stables right next to the farm,
When young children ride me I'm placid and calm.
I'm steadfast and strong when put through my paces,
It's worth it to see the smiles on their faces.

For horse shows I'm groomed and stand very proud,
When I jump a clear round I'm clapped by the crowd,
I will get a rosette if all goes well.
It's my turn now at the sound of the bell.

Suzannah Ecclestone (14)
Rising Brook High School

SUMMER TIME

The clouds are so high
in the blue sky
where the seagulls fly.

The seaside is so noisy in the day
But when it turns to night
It goes silent and you just hear the deep blue
sea sway.

When it's a bright sunny day
People are happy in all kinds of ways
On a summer's day.

Donna Parsons (14)
Rising Brook High School

CHARLES AND DIANA

Hugs and kisses all around
A perfect couple
Can be found
Throughout the palace of the town

All the crowds were there
So sweet and fair
The best marriage of the year
In 1981

All the crowds clapped and cheered
It sounded like a clap of thunder
The perfect couple will never die
Because they are so much in love

The wedding is no more
No Charles and Diana for sure
All the smiles gone to waste
In 1996

A perfect couple no more
A divorce is held
Poor Charles and Diana
It wasn't meant to be
In 1996

Charles is still with Camilla
Diana is rich
They got what they wanted
In 1996.

Lorna Barnett (12)
Rising Brook High School

ALIEN NATION OFF ITS TROLLEY!

Viewing TV all weekend,
I walked to work with pleasure,
Beneath the bridge I spotted,
Wheels sticking out the river.

I approached Riverside Centre,
Wheeled monsters were everywhere,
Had the Daleks returned to earth?
I was scared, I gave a shiver.

What could I do, I asked myself?
The mist began to clear.
The Daleks suddenly metamorphosed,
Into shopping trolleys.

No-one saw me, I don't think,
I went to work with devilish thoughts,
I worked all day but not a word,
but it slipped to the back of my mind.

Walking home by council office,
I saw trolleys; millions and billions,
Were they attacking the Civic HQ?
Ha! I laughed that's life!

Having just awoke from alien tests,
I hear a voice loud and clear,
It's something that to me sounds like:
'We will exterminate Staffordshire.'

Now I am hearing something else,
'We tried to invade Wildwood,
but they kept taking us back to Tesco's,
to get their one pound coin back.'

Matthew Long (13)
Rising Brook High School

BADGER'S FIGHT FOR LIFE

In the heart of the country,
The still of the night,
The badger is foraging,
Coat black and white
He shuffles around,
Unaware of his fate,
Not knowing that someone
Will hunt him for bait.
For the innocent creature
Life can be unfair,
He might end his days
In a trap or a snare,
Or under the wheels of a car -
Who will care?
Thank goodness for people
Who like them alive,
With groups who are working
To help them survive.
They help them and nurse them
With funds that they get,
So badgers can live safe and sound in their set.

Sarah Thompson (12)
Rising Brook High School

Dog In A Pet Shop

I'd love to go to a nice cosy home,
Where I'll get a lot of tender loving care,
And I won't be alone.

Rusty the glossy cocker-spaniel,
Was snapped up by a young lad called Daniel.
Who took him home to fuss and pamper,
For nothing would that dog hanker.

Lucky the silky golden Labrador,
Was taken by a girl called Eleanor,
She brought him a collar and a brand new dish,
And she panders to his every wish.

A scruffy little mongrel like me,
With big paws and a scrawny tail,
Who's as ugly as ugly can be . . .
My future's plain to see . . .

I'd love to go to a nice cosy home,
Where I'll get a lot of tender loving care,
And I won't be alone.

Tracey Shore (13)
Rising Brook High School

I Once Had A Sister

I have a sister who's football mad,
I guess she got it from my dad.

The Magpies are her favourite team,
In black and white they play a dream.

All day long she kicked the ball,
Until she smashed the garden wall.

She'd got nothing to kick the ball against
So then she started using the fence.

Dad went mad and sent her packing
And said in sense she was lacking

How she wished that she lived nearer,
To her hero Alan Shearer.

Sally Kendrick (12)
Rising Brook High School

THE BALD EAGLE

Swift and steady I shall fly,
All the way right up to the sky
Searching for food to settle my hunger,
As I fly I feel so much younger.

As I arrive at my mountain top eyrie
The air crisp and clear, I see very clearly.
As I glance down through the tall trees,
Something catches my sight, down on its knees.

The deep black funnel sidled towards me,
It shuffled slightly and then raised one knee.
I heard a click and then came blackness,
Once hit the ground my wings became flightless.

Silence lingered in the deep wood,
Autumn leaves were stained in deep blood.
No creatures scuttled, no birds sang,
This was the cause of the ear piercing bang.

Sarah Murray (13)
Rising Brook High School

THE SNOWMAN

I built a snowman
I call him Mr Snow

When I got back to the classroom,
I heard a noise oh no.

I saw Mr Snow moving,
Then he actually walked.

Slowly he walked towards me.

He stopped and raised his hat.
But he fell and *splat!*

He was nothing
        but a little heap of snow.

Matthew Fletcher (14)
Rocklands School

AUTUMN

Autumn leaves drift to the ground
Silently land without a sound
Leaves crunch under your feet
And make a nice crispy carpet seat.

I hear the wind howling down my lane,
It doesn't at all sound the same
As the summer sunny days
As each tree gently sways.

Autumn days are dull and wet
And that lovely sunset
Orange, yellow and red
Nearly all the plants are now dead.

All the animals start to hibernate
Some even leave their mate
Squirrels busily gathering nuts
Conkers fall into deep ruts.

James Hiam (9)
St Giles Church of England School

THE STARS

The stars are clipped meteors
Floating through the sky.

Floating past shooting stars
That zoom through the sky.

But that's not in the daytime
They come out at night.

They shine, they shine
Sparkling for you and me!

Katie Mansfield (12)
St Thomas More Catholic College

A View From A Hill

I hear a crunching of the leaves,
It sounds like big trees,
I see a person down below,
They look like creepy crawling ants,
I see a bird flying past,
Was it a bird or was it a cat?
I smell the trees and damp damp soil,
I hear an ambulance rushing past,
It look so nice from up so high,
I see a house or is it a mouse?
Oh there's that cow I smelt him pass.

Dawn Shenton (11)
St Thomas More Catholic College

Question And Answer

What is the sky made of?
The sky is blue candy floss,
What is the moon made of?
The moon is white milk chocolate,
Where are babies found?
babies are found on the doorstep,
Where is God?
God is eating the candy floss,
What are clouds?
Clouds are the holes in the sky that God has eaten.

Adam Rowson (11)
St Thomas More Catholic College

PARACHUTE JUMPING

It's my turn now,
What if my parachute doesn't work,
What happens if it gets caught,
The only thing going to happen is,
I'm falling, falling and gone.

The landscape below me is coming nearer,
It looks like squares and rectangles
From a board game,
And all the people look like little insects.

When I was falling through the air,
You can feel the wind in your face,
And you think you are in a race,
That is the sensation of falling.

The last few seconds that I floated to earth,
Felt that everything came before me,
I wish that I could do it again.

Samantha Housley (12)
St Thomas More Catholic College

A VIEW FROM A HILL

From the top of the hill I can see;
A flying little buzzing bee.

A housing estate in Parkhall,
A field and a bit of rubble.

A patch of trees, a lake too,
But best of all are the big big hills.

Gordon Parton (12)
St Thomas More Catholic College

THE JUMP!

The plane is climbing up so high
Now I'm above the clouds.

Do I really want to jump?
Do I really want to die?

Look out of the window,
At the landscape below.

Do I really want to jump?
Do I really have to die?

What if the parachute doesn't open?
What if the earth comes to fast?

Do I really have to jump?
Do I really have to die?

Now I'm floating in the sky
My parachute has opened and
Now I won't die.

Amy Day (12)
St Thomas More Catholic College

FREE FALL

Falling falling ever faster
parachute doesn't open
falling falling ever faster
hit the ground need a plaster.

Philip Bates (12)
St Thomas More Catholic College

A View From A Hill

I see a big fat bus crawling along the road,
barging its way through all the traffic.
Chimney smoke oozing out of factories,
like steam coming out of a kettle,
I see people queuing to go into the shops,
people in shops are all packed like sardines in a tin.
I see police cars chasing criminals,
fire engines roaring along the road with sirens blaring,
I see fumes coming out of cars,
like water coming out of a burst pipe.
Most of all I can smell a chip shop a mile away.

Ashley Gouldsmith (11)
St Thomas More Catholic College

Animals

I like animals big and bold as
long as they do as they are told.

I like animals that can walk
I only wish they could talk.

I like animals big and small
some hairy some bald.

I like animals that like
to bark and protect me
in the dark.

Anthony Evans (12)
St Thomas More Catholic College

ON MY ISLAND

I stand there picking the
money off the large fully
grown trees,
I do what I like on my
island,
Drinking,
eating,
Dancing,
What fun.
Just me alone,
No-one to talk to,
How peaceful,
Maybe I could take a
break in a Coca-Cola
lake.

Sarah Hughes (11)
St Thomas More Catholic College

FREE FALL

A fall from a plane
Can be very insane

The ground is like
A chess board from up there!

The fall is free
But you might
Hit a tree

That's why it's not for me!

Samantha Jones (11)
St Thomas More Catholic College

BIRTHDAYS

Birthdays are only once a year. I
wish it were more,
It could be twice or five times or
maybe thirty more,
Opening all the presents,
Also blowing out the candles on the
cake,
Whether you're eleven, thirteen or fifteen,
You should still have fun,
I love birthdays don't you.

Kirsty Grattage (12)
St Thomas More Catholic College

THE GREAT TRAIN

Come onto my train
My great train
My special train that flies.
It flies up into the high sky
It flies to other planets
Up in space you can relax
with sweets, chocolates and drinks
You can get sweets from
the sweet planet
All the clouds are candyfloss,
The sun is made out of drink
The moon is made out of cheese
So everything is great on
              the great train.

Simon Carter (12)
St Thomas More Catholic College

WAR REMEMBRANCE

In the trenches the defence is
strong,
People being slaughtered all night
long,
Soldiers fought to death,
blood and guts flying everywhere,
Britain is devouring everything
in its path.

Craig Slater (13)
St Thomas More Catholic College

MY DREAM

I'm going to the jet plane,
flying here and there.
Oh! yes it's only my dream.
I'd like to fly a jet plane
flying in the sky,
I won't be back for tea till I've
finished my flight.

I'd like to fly a jet plane
high above the stars
Oh! Yes I forgot it's only my dream.
I'd love to be a pilot with my smart
suit.

I'd like to fly a jet plane all
around the world.
Oh! I forgot it's only my dream.
I'd love to be a pilot with my smart cap.
But when I wake up it was only my dream.

Jenna Wootton (12)
St Thomas More Catholic College

WHY IS THERE WAR?

Is this war going to end?
Will the world be able to mend
Will we be able to tend soldiers' wounds
Bang, bang is all we heard
My children cry at a bang
Oh, please God tell me why
Can we have peace once more

This world was so peaceful
Before the war
Everyone was happy
But look what's happened
No-one is happy, just sad
One little girl said 'I miss my dad'
I wonder why this war started
And all the children have darted
Far, far away
Away from their family.
But they can only wait
I wonder, I wonder why
If we can stop this war
Come on we can try
Then there will be peace once more.

Clare Davis (12)
St Thomas More Catholic College

THE ICED MOUNTAINS

The wind blows a breeze through
The Slush puppy trees
The jelly babies frown as they fall to
the ground bowing before me on their
knees,
All the people are nice.
All the rivers and waterfalls are chocolate,
All the plants are lollipops on sticks,
Everything's free they all grow on one tree,
All the clouds are made of candy floss.
The sun is a giant lemon sherbet,
My house is a big mass of toffee.
But the part you'll like best more
than all the rest is the big ice
cream mountains.

Paul Storey (13)
St Thomas More Catholic College

DREAM ON

Last night I was dreaming again
about what I would do
if I lived in a dreamland
where nothing mattered, nothing
at all.
It's like a wonderland that
seems so small.
the sun is always shining
all of the time.
If only I would be able to
know that this land is
mine all mine.

Samantha Goodwin (12)
St Thomas More Catholic College

My Dream

Gazing through my window
Looking all around
I can hear birds singing
See flowers blooming
The dog running through
The leaves that dropped
Crunch, crunch, crunch

Gazing through my window
Looking all around
Looking at the pond
Then by the corner of my eye
I saw a fountain running like
A waterfall
That is my dream
Please come true.

Stephanie Filcock (12)
St Thomas More Catholic College

My Parachute Jump

My heart was beating fast,
as the helicopter took off,
I had strange feelings,
that my parachute wouldn't open,
that something goes wrong with the helicopter,
I leapt out of the helicopter,
I couldn't find my cord to pull,
I was feeling weak all of a sudden,
then I found my cord and pulled it.

Lesley Cadman (12)
St Thomas More Catholic College

HEAVEN AND EARTH

I think of my heaven as blue as
the sea
Sitting on the clouds laughing
with my friends and family.
Waterfalls falling like rain from
the sky
Not afraid of anything because
I know God is near by.
Angels shining as bright as the
sun
Everybody is laughing and having fun.
Thank you God for creating earth
Thank you God for creating birth.
You made families you made
friends
You made love that never ends.

Rebecca Carrick (12)
St Thomas More Catholic College

THE SKY

The sky.
She always changes her mind.
When she's happy,
she smiles.
When she's sad,
she cries.
And the birds always fly in the sky.
The birds like her,
flowers need her,
everybody likes her,
and we love her.

Raymond Lam (14)
St Thomas More Catholic College

F A Cup Dream

I wish I walked down
Wembley Way, where all
the flags were waving all
the way. We suddenly stepped
upon the pitch and if we won
we would be rich. We suddenly
ran up the wing and then
the crowd started to sing.

I crossed it in, heads went
in, as the ball slowly dropped
in. The time had come for us
to win as the ref put the
whistle into his mouth . . . and
slowly but surely the cup
was ours.

Robert McGuire (12)
St Thomas More Catholic College

Fire V Water

The fire has started,
it's burning and crackling,
but here comes the water
and it's on.
The fire begins to sizzle
oh no the fire is going out
going, going, gone!
It's out and it's over within
minutes.
The water is the winner.

Vicky Davies (12)
St Thomas More Catholic College

PEACE AND QUIET

Peace and quiet
there is no riot
this is heaven
there is no war.

Peace would be nice
just as quiet as mice
where people just laugh and play.
There would not be a price to pay.
War is not a token
friendship is never broken.

People would not be broken
they would not be noisy, upset
and sad.
Friends and family happy and
glad.
Friends are forever
Don't have war
It's not what people are
for.
It's painful and sore
      just like war.

Siobhan Daly (12)
St Thomas More Catholic College

MY LITTLE FLY

I open my eyes early in the morning,
I look out of the window,
and what do I see,
Birds, cats, dogs.
Trees swaying side to side.
I look up into the sky,
And there I see a helpless
little fly.
So I reach out of the window
and put it in a jar,
And then I say,
Oh, my, oh, my, you are my
little star.
Goodbye, my little fly.

Rachel Dawson (12)
St Thomas More Catholic College

PARACHUTE JUMP

My heart was pounding like a big bass drum
My legs were trembling right to the bone
My family were saying it will be fantastic
What do they know?

As the aeroplane took off
I heard this voice inside me saying 'No don't do this'
But my family are standing on the ground expecting me to do this.

It was my turn.
I froze at the door then somebody pushed me.
My parachute opened thank goodness
My parents were overjoyed
I was just glad to be on the ground.

Kerrie Evans (12)
St Thomas More Catholic College

FIRE V WATER

And the battle's begun!

Splish! Splash! Water splashes Fire
Almost knocked him out
Burn, sparkle whoosh!
Fire gets angry
Fire starts to flash back
Running towards water they
Both bounce back from each other
In instant shock!
Water got up again
Jumped on a high level
And bounced onto Fire
And burned him out!

Rhian Weston (12)
St Thomas More Catholic College

PARADISE

Paradise for me is a
wonderful island.
The sun is shining and there's
a clear crystal sea.
With a cave full of chocolate
and money growing on trees.
With beautiful birds with colourful
feathers. With no schools and no
rules. Mermaids swimming in the sea
and having fun with me.
With no-one doing any work.
We all eat chocolate and drink
chocolate. It certainly is paradise
for me.

Fazana Khurshid (12)
St Thomas More Catholic College

THE BIG RACE LIVE
SUN V MOON

Welcome to the big race live!
The Sun is in pole position,
With Moon second on the grid,
Remember when the 3 red lights
Go out the race will begin.
Three light are on
They have gone out
It is go!

The Sun is being tightly raced out,
Birds sing, flowers are about.
The Moon tries getting past
It is an eclipse.

But the Sun is still in front
Here comes the Moon
And the Moon gets past,
Owls awake, people asleep.

The Moon crosses the line in front.
With Sun second
And Cloud third.

The Moon wins, it's night
Till later goodbye!

Ben Sims (12)
St Thomas More Catholic College

FIRE VS WATER

It's nearly full-time
Here at the bonfire
It's 1-1
Water is putting on the
Pressure
But wait
Fire is making
A sparkling run.
He puts in a cross
In comes an explosion
It's a smashing header
It's too hot to handle.
A goal 2-1
It's kick off
There's less than four minutes left!
Here comes a wave of a cross
It hits the back of the net
One minute left a run past
Everybody it's a goaaal! They're
Going in, in waves full-time a
Splash win for Water.

Kieran Bevan (12)
St Thomas More Catholic College

PARACHUTE JUMP

When I look down from the sky,
I feel my stomach turn over
like a washing machine.

When I jump out into
the sky,
I feel as light as a
feather,

The land I see is like
a checked waistcoat,
but it is just the
fields,

At the last few seconds when
I pull the string,
I feel myself floating down
I position myself for
   landing.

Stefan Rouch (12)
St Thomas More Catholic College

MY PARADISE ISLAND

My paradise is a place
where money grows on
trees,
with chocolate seas and
honey bees.
There is no school and no
strict rules on the island
that's for me.
The grass stays green,
the sky stays blue
and no one gets the
flu.
There will be maids running
after you.
And only a few people will
do,
on the island for me and
you.

Isabella Angotti (12)
St Thomas More Catholic College

PARACHUTE POEM

I'm waiting for my jump

>One go
>Two go

The man shouted,
>>another three and I go

One
   Two
      Three

>I'm pushed
> what a feeling

I pulled the cord

>my parachute opens

All's going well when

>*Crash*

I'm hanging from a tree and shouting

>*Help me!*

Russell Dimmock (13)
St Thomas More Catholic College

PARACHUTE JUMP

The surrounding air is pushing you forward,
As the door of the aeroplane opens.
The first dives out and shouts very loud,
The second daren't go.
It's my turn now I'm all tensed up,
I'm nervous all my body is shaking.

>*Jump!*

Whooaaa!

50 maybe 60 miles per hour,
This is amazing.
Faster than a bird flying through the sky,
The landscape looks like a big blanket.
The land is near I've reached the ground,
My fear is over and never will be found.

Alan Rosenau (12)
St Thomas More Catholic College

MY PARACHUTE JUMP

We climbed 1000 feet,
Then 4000 feet,
Then 10000 feet,

The door opened,
My heart stopped,

Then the light went amber,
Then green,

I was floating like a feather in the sky,
I looked down,
My world like ants in the grass,
Then it grew bigger and bigger,

I pulled my cord,
My parachute opened
I floated down even slower

Then bang I've hit the ground,
The parachute comes over me like a cloud,
Then I want to do it again.

Simon Dowling (12)
St Thomas More Catholic College

FISH

People learn to swim,
it seems such a sin
We belong to the land
To live safe on the sand
Because no matter how
you tried, you never would
succeed. The fish would never
heed. On how to walk the
land.

Stephen Snee (12)
St Thomas More Catholic College

CHOCOLATE ISLAND

I am a chocoholic
I eat it every day,
I'd have my dream island
filled with Wispa Gold,
with one or two waterfalls running near by.

The sea would be smothered
with chocolate like a relaxing mud pool.
My island would be for only chocoholics,
people like me!
The sand would be as gold as caramel,
the tree branches and trunks would be as brown as
chocolate, and the grass as green as an unripe tomato.
The sky would always be blue, with twittering birds
flying by.
This is definitely my paradise island.

Lianne Jones (12)
St Thomas More Catholic College

THE MOON

I'm a moon
I'm a moon
swinging like a
baby's cradle high
in the sky.
Watching over the
people below.
As they sleep
eat and live
on the world down
there below.

Clare Parkes (13)
St Thomas More Catholic College

WAR POETRY

You could hear the bangs for miles
around,
and the thick, black smoke covered like a
cloud.
You could see the fear in all men's faces
but they knew they were fighting for their
places.
They lost their lives for what they
believed,
but their families' sorrow would never be
relieved.
Men that came back alive and well, were
faced with fear from that unlucky spell.
Now for them, we pray and remember,
On the eleventh hour, on the eleventh of
November.

Donna Beer (15)
St Thomas More Catholic College

THE SHOOTING STAR

Now and again I see a star
Shooting high over my head.
When it comes over it looks
to me as if it was nearly touching my bed.
The star that I see shivers with glee
over the moonlit sky.
Sometimes, if no-one is looking, I
would even wave goodbye!
The star at night is very bright
as I see it go over my house.
I would even say that this star
was as quiet as a mouse.
The glistening, silvery star,
looks just like the sparkling
tinsel upon a Christmas tree
as it flies away, when night
in bed soon becomes day.

Richard Bell (12)
St Thomas More Catholic College

NO-ONE CAN EVER KNOW

The mud is starting to go hard on
My skin and clothes.
The trenches are full of dead bodies
The sight of this no-one can ever know.
I hope and pray, each night of each day
That the war will be over soon.
When I go home,
There will be someone to go home to.

Claire Pyatt (14)
St Thomas More Catholic College

A Star

A star is a man who could not breathe
A man who could not walk
A man whose life was pointless . . .
But one day the man asked God Almighty
To end his life on earth
The Lord God agreed to this one thing
And then right on the spot
Beamed the man up to the galaxies
There the man had a purpose to live
It was to act as God's light
And show other people the way.

Isaac Maxwell (12)
St Thomas More Catholic College

Dresden

The sirens screech in the night,
And planes soar overhead,
The you hear a gentle whistle,
The sky is red and the ground is yellow and
All you can hear is screaming!

The tanks rumble through the streets,
Crushing all in sight,
And soldiers run shouting,
People are under mounds of rock,
The floor painted red with blood.

And there you are,
One eye open, one eye closed.
You can hear them but they can't hear you,
Everything goes black and at last you hear
Boom! Boom! Bang!

Steven Booth (14)
St Thomas More Catholic College

CONTESTANT POEM

Here we are sports fans
At the big fight live!
We've got Night versus Light.

And here we go sports fans,
It's Night the champion
And Light the challenger.

The first punch comes from Light,
But Night gets in a few left right combinations,
And knocks Light down,
But he's up.

Night gets some punches in,
But Light gets in a beautiful left hook,
Light continues the punishment,
And Night's going, going gone.

1, 2, 3, 4, 5, 6, 7, 8, 9, 10.
Light's the winner of the championship.
But Night will be back.

Russell Ball (12)
St Thomas More Catholic College

IN THE END, IT'S THERE AGAIN

The Paras were trooping,
landing over enemy lines.
Their concrete packs pull them to
the ground, whilst artillery shells destroy
once used buildings. To them, it's now
an unheard sound.

Marines file out of personnel carriers,
into sludge which lies below.
Under the cover of darkness, they move,
with heavy weapons in tow.

The special unit: Navy seals, not the
arctic sort:
Bravely fighting battles they never should
have fought. Disregarding their safety,
to serve their country well, body count
next morning, reveals the need for the
knelling bell.

Dean Quinn (14)
St Thomas More Catholic College

HELPLESS IN WAR

We marched to war,
It was said to be our duty
Our mourning wives and
Our helpless children we left behind.

We struggled out of muddy trenches
With lifeless people lying at my feet,
Some of them with bloody gashes crying
Out for help clinging on to the last
Minutes of life dying without their dignity.

We won that war but I feel remorse.
I watched my friends die at my feet.
Writhing up like dying poppies.
Poppies the flower for justice
But there was no justice served
In this war.
The glamorised picture of war
Still shines through.

Kim Hollins (14)
St Thomas More Catholic College

THE LAND OF DREAMS

The land of dreams
is a money one where
money grows on trees

There will be no school
no strict rules no
teachers there to tell
me off

The sea shall be chocolate
the lakes shall be Coke
that shall be the dream
island for me.

Hayley Miller (13)
St Thomas More Catholic College

MODERN WAR

Tanks, planes and trucks
Bullets, bombs, and explosions,
Dead bodies being cleaned away,
Bloodstains still mark the spots where they lay,

Green, black and brown
The colours of the camouflage,
Everything must blend in,
One little thing may result in death.

In fifty years, things have come a long way,
So why won't war go away.

Dominic Salt (14)
St Thomas More Catholic College

IMAGE OF WAR

Trudging along,
Over bodies of blood,
Only one thought on their minds,
Getting through it alive.

Bombs blasting,
Guns firing,
Bodies mounting up,
All lying in pools of blood.

At last it's ended,
Mounds of people,
Pools of blood,
And families left distraught.

Cheryl Smith (14)
St Thomas More Catholic College

DEATH

Death conquers all
Taking everything in
its path
Ripping families apart

Death conquers all
Marching for days
like cattle on the move.
Waiting at night ready
to blow
Ready for the silence
to turn to rage
When that life threatening
battle comes.

Matthew Miller (15)
St Thomas More Catholic College

WAR

The mindless chatter
of a nearby machine gun,
rings in your ears.
A mix of civilians
and heavily armed soldiers
running for cover.
Napalm exploding
with every step.
Bodies of the unfortunate,
Slung in the gutter.
Limbs trampled, and
grotesquely altered,
by a stampeding mass of people.
Weapons extensions of bodies,
callously killing innocent strangers.
Where Harpy meets Neanderthal,
and people die as a result.
A slice of Armageddon.

Abigail Dodd (14)
St Thomas More Catholic College

FAT CATS

The generals sit there,
drinking their wine, dining
in the best hotels
sending men off to die
what right have they?

While they wine and dine
men die like slaughtered swine
it's nice, cosy and tasteful or
bad, bloody and hateful.

They are the fat cats
Soldiers are the rats.
Fat cats prey on the rats
and send them into the
battle zone to die.

But what do they do to help?

David Bates (14)
St Thomas More Catholic College

WAR

Sitting back at their posh desks,
Polishing their medals.
Whilst on the front line,
those new recruits,
In dirty, bloody, war-torn suits.
Limping on without pain or fear,
Not even stopping to shed a tear.
Or thinking of the grey haired
Major,
Who takes the honour,
And the glory,
Of this life-long story.
War!

Francis Murphy (14)
St Thomas More Catholic College

F-16 Red 3

They flew in the boiling sun
Knowing war was not a lot of fun.
Flying high above the sandy earth
in their F-16s battle weary and tired
enough as to not notice three Migs
flying up to get 'em!

'Look low Jackson! Migs at 6 low.'
The three F-16s panicked and turned
and turned and whirled round
to dodge the side-winders homing
on the heat of the engines.

They missed. Only three *bang!*
only two got away. Only one
F-16 red 3 was left behind to
tumble and spin and spin like
a merry-go-round, to the ground
with an enormous pound into the
earth.

F-16 1 and 2 'ran' like men running from
a mad bull.
In their fear of death and being killed
they knew that F-16 red 3 had been killed.

The Migs circled the wreck and circled
like vultures over meat
and knew they had no defeat
but that they had victory!

Adam Grannell (15)
St Thomas More Catholic College

CHRISTMAS

A season of joy
A season of love
A season of happiness
Is this enough
>Lots of children
>This time is no fun
>No mom or dad
>To give them love

Sadness fills their hearts
Brings a tear to their eye
As once again
Santa walks by.

>No-one cares
>No-one knows
>They sit and cry
>As another year passes by.

They sit and weep
A tear drops to their feet
They hope and pray
They can survive another day.

Anne-Marie Boulstridge (13)
The Rawlett School

THE WEIRD AND WEARY HOUSE

Dark and weary:
There's a ghost behind the door;
Thump goes the mirror all in pieces on the floor;
Click goes the TV it's been turned on;
Bash goes the shed door opening and closing;
That's our house in pieces on the floor:

Mark Dayton (11)
The Rawlett School

THE MIDNIGHT ROOM

When midnight strikes, out it comes . . .
The bells hit twelve and then . . .
The horrid feeling of something cold
shivers down my spine.
Is it really a ghost nobody knows.
But then no-one dares to enter the
Midnight room.
Where there in that room something lurks
waiting in our presence.
But nobody dares to enter that Midnight
room.
For it may only be a rat or a mouse
that makes this horrid noise.
I wonder what it might be in that
Midnight room.

Holly Sadler (12)
The Rawlett School

THE STIRRING HOUSE

On a light night the moon shone bright,
Down in the world below a house would glow,
A woman is stirring in her bed,
Endlessly trying to sleep.
The woman gets up thuddedy thud,
Down the stairs she climbs.
Awoken by all the commotion,
A man turns grumbles and groans,
The woman downstairs, sitting at a red hot stove,
Still chewing the woman comes upstairs,
In to bed she pops and all is asleep.

Hannah Martin (11)
The Rawlett School

THE TURN OF THE CLOCK

As the witching hour slowly draws near,
A deathly silence drifts through the still air.
Now is the time in the death of night,
That darkness overpowers light.

The warm crackling fire no longer blazing,
The sound of the street cars no longer racing.
No sound of tiny mice scurrying along the kitchen floor,
Not even the sound of everyday callers knocking
                                    persistently at the door.
There is no creaking of a key turning in the lock,
There is absolute silence until the turn of the clock.

As the witching hour, slowly draws near,
A deathly silence drifts through the still air.
Now is the time in the death of night,
That darkness overpowers light . . .

Sophie Horrobin (12)
The Rawlett School

RIVER ISLAND

I like to shop, shop till I drop
In the store I push and shove
Fighting for the clothes I love.

There on the rack is just what I need
Two sizes too small! I want it all the more!

In the changing room hot and sticky
You can bet it's going to be tricky.

The price is steep but what the heck
I'll look good you can bet!

Annabelle Rowley (13)
The Rawlett School

What Happened To Summer?

As I stare out of the window into the icy cold
I wonder where summer's gone, with its colours bright and bold
It's as if autumn is a curse made through the night
My garden now a delicate, but empty sight
The leaves turn golden brown, die, then fall to the ground
Drifting slowly down like a feather, without making a single sound
They make a carpet on the grass, of yellow, russet and red
Devious autumn kidnapped summer while we were all in bed
With his sidekick Jack Frost, who is everywhere you go
What's happened to summer? That's all we want to know
Those beating rays on your back
Instead of cold-hearted Jack
The one we know, the one we hate
Why couldn't autumn have turned up late
Where summer has gone, nobody knows, we all have our own pictures
in our head
Will summer be back? Is it sleeping? Or maybe it is dead.

Marie Jealous (14)
The Rawlett School

Death Row

He went to the sink to wash for the last time.
The sink was dirty and covered in grime.
His family visited to say their goodbyes.
And as he left tears filled their eyes.
He went to the small church full of remorse.
His stomach was churning and his throat felt hoarse.
He stepped into the room and looked around.
All was silent there wasn't a sound.
They strapped in his arms legs and head
And with a flick of a switch so quickly he's dead.

Andrew Turner (13)
The Rawlett School

THE FIRES OF HELL

I'm sitting in this festering trench,
It has the most disgusting stench,
It smells of earth, the dying and the dead,
A murky morass is my bed.

I pray I will forget the things I've seen,
and return to the way things once had been,
The shelling sounds like claps of thunder,
Ploughing the enemy's barbed wire under.

The shelling has stopped,
Is the war over?
Will I return to my home in Dover?

The war is not over, but much worse still,
The generals say we must capture a hill,
We must march out in the dead of night,
We must battle and we must fight,
We must march towards the Huns,
Under fire from machine guns.

The ladders are up,
The whistle is blown,
Out of our trench, my company's thrown,
Into the storm of bullet and shell,
That roars like the raging fires of Hell.

Chris Killeen (13)
The Rawlett School

GROWTH

A seed, sown by the hand of life,
Lying deep beneath the earth,
May grow to reach the stars one day,
Or shrivel and die at birth.

That one seed, sleeping in the ground,
Awakes from its slumber to sprout,
To grow with care, and learn to love,
And to learn what life is about.

Like a snake's old skin, the seed is shed
Letting the plant within grow free,
For contained in this amazing seed,
Is the future for us to see.

As time progresses, the plant grows old,
Wrinkled and shrivelled and slow,
Until one day the dreaded time comes
With a feeling of sorrow and woe.

For the time comes for all of us,
The time we get is not a lot,
There is a lesson to be learnt,
Make use of the time you have got.

Mark Demain (13)
The Rawlett School

SNOW

Snowflakes falling to the ground,
Drifting slowly like white feathers all around,

Clinging softly to a tree,
One by one they foam like sea,

Soft and crunchy underfoot,
Glistening and silvery a glance is all it took,

Children making snowmen full of fun,
As slowly as it arrived out came the sun,

One by one you see them disappear,
And the children's eyes fill with a tear.

Jason Reid (13)
The Rawlett School

THE RAINFOREST

I walk through the rainforest,
Sun in the sky,
Looking around wondering why?
Why is it so beautiful to the human eye.

All of a sudden a parrot flies by,
Why is the rainforest going to die?
It is so quiet to you and I.

I see a beautiful bird in the trees,
I see some fish in a lake swimming by,
I stand and wonder why?
Why does the wildlife have to die.

Sam Collins (13)
The Rawlett School

AT THE MATCH

As we go through the stadium door,
We feel like royalty as the crowd begin to roar.
Then I realise that the footballers are about to start,
The last match of the season between Celtic and Hearts.
Scarves and banners are waving in the air,
As fans chant to show that they care.
Celtic's tackling is very rough,
Which makes the ref get very tough.
With a sending off and a booking too,
The crowd responds with a big loud *boo*!
It's half-time and a 0-0 score,
The managers tell them that they are playing poor.
'Back to work and let's get scoring,
We don't want this match to turn boring.'
They're back on the pitch playing for the cup,
As the cheerleaders try to bring good luck.
Celtic have the ball and it hurtles into the net,
If the score stays like this then I've won the bet.
The dreaded whistle is blown and it's all over,
I've definitely won so I'm going to Dover!

Rebecca Patten (13)
The Rawlett School

RUGBY

Kicking balls through the post,
I wonder which team will get the most
The scrum-half, puts the ball in
While the hooker is mostly maulin'

The referee stops the play
The pack train everyday
The stand-off gets the ball
Passes it to the great, Eric Hall

The number nine is so small.
I wonder how he gets the ball
The ball is kicked out of play,
They practise this, everyday

The whistle goes the fans all cheer;
I'll meet you in the bar for a beer
The game is over, the fans go home,
The groundsmen are busy, all alone.

Neil Orton (13)
The Rawlett School

TRAMP

Oi get out of the way
I heard them say
find another place to camp
you smelly old tramp
we ain't got time for you!

People stare, kids point and glare
that is why I'm in this mess
cause no-one treats me fair
I guess it's not really their fault
I'm the one to blame
if I'd helped my family out
then they wouldn't have been in
the flames
But now that they have gone
I haven't a family of my own
I only need a few more pence
to buy me a scrap of ham on a bone
I know that shortly soon I shall die
and that there shall not be one
tear in one's eyes.

Victoria Masters (13)
The Rawlett School

HUMAN KIND

All us humans are in a race,
let's all settle in a decent pace.
Some people think that God made us,
We travel by car, train and bus.

We all have hands, a face and feet,
through all these places we lose heat.
Heart, liver, kidney and a brain,
all of our energy these will drain.

Will human kind destroy this earth,
by giving nature a wide berth.
Old fashioned morals can we revive,
so that human kind can survive.

Andrew Hough (14)
The Rawlett School

CHRISTMAS DAY!

It's Christmas, it's Christmas,
The children run downstairs.
To see what Santa's left them;
And see what the presents bear!

Wrapping paper's all over the floor,
As well as a half eaten apple core!
The scent of turkey and pine,
Fills the room, once again.

The family gather round to eat,
The sight of turkey; what a treat!
As the father carves the meat;
They all sit down in their special seat!

Louise Hodgetts (13)
The Rawlett School

FOOTBALL

On Sunday afternoon, I am all set,
Because on Sunday afternoon I have a
football match.
When everyone gets down to the pitch,
All the players have to have a good stretch.

After half an hour of warm up,
The two captains have to toss up,
And we have a kick with Dave and Mack
Suddenly we make pressure with a strong
attack.

Spreading the ball side to side,
Forcing the defence to even our glide,
The ball glides in like a boulder,
With Dave scoring somehow with his shoulder.

We're one nil up and ten minutes to go
With Rangers forcing us but very slow.
We gain possession and pass about.
Us waiting for the ref to whistle out

The ref blows the whistle and we all cheer,
With George running on with all the beer,
We all go home to have our showers,
waiting till next week to beat the 'Towers'.

Gary Marston (13)
The Rawlett School

A Rabbit

Hopping around the cage outside,
The rabbit jumps from side to side,
Eating her food she jumps about,
Hoping to get out with no doubt.

Letting her out the cage she runs free.
Running around the garden she hides behind the tree,
Hopping and jumping around all day,
The rabbit settles down from her play.

Going back in her cage to go to sleep,
All night long there isn't a peep,
Dreaming of wonderful things,
Wondering what they could bring.

Becky Newman (14)
The Rawlett School

Snow

White as a pure bit of paper,
Covering everything in sight,
Like a big fluffy blanket.

I walk with excitement,
Leaving my footprints in the snow,
I feel alone in the snow.

It's a race to get to the snow first,
To make a footprint,
It's fun to walk in the snow.

It's time to go home now,
Oh why do I have to,
Please let me see more and stay.

Pamela Heafield (12)
The Rawlett School

GRAND PRIX

The engines rev up.
The start is near.
The noise of the engines is all you can hear.
The colourful cars are on the grid.
This could be the main race for your championship bid.

The mechanics clear the circuit.
Now it's time to show you're worth it.
Red turns to green.
The crowd scream.
They turn the first corner, they're no longer to be seen.

10 laps left.
The cars are zooming by.
Second and first place are near by.
They go into the pit.
Who will come out first.
One's had to retire his tyres burst.

Last lap! It's gone down to the wire.
Final corner, one of the engines has set on fire.
It's a race to the line.
Red or blue who will win.
The blue driver puts his foot down.
The chequered flags waved around.

Simon Griffiths (13)
The Rawlett School

GLIDER

Smoothly, slowly, gliding down,
Silently, swiftly to the ground.
Faster and faster circling round.
Through a thermal, with a gust,
Up, up, up and up,
Through the clouds,
Free as a bird, no sound.

Lots of planes pass you by,
Further and further up in the sky
See the world from a bird's eye view,
Some sheep and farms too.
Then slowly you begin your descent,
Air brakes on, nose dipping,
Stomach churning.

Then, you can breathe freely,
You feel very safe.
Silently you drift down,
With a gentle thud, hit the ground.
The experience is over, all is calm.
You sit there thinking,
Sweat on your palms.
What it was like to be free,
You sit back and chuckle with glee.

James Allsopp (13)
The Rawlett School

WIMBLEDON

Life absorbed in all players on court,
Returning the yellow dot which has fallen short,

The burning ball above magnifies the
one below,
Both zapping energy from the players,

Sweat sprays onto the short grass.
Like a shower from the threatening clouds,

Players on court hear 'Deuce!' at 40 all.
Desperate for drinks to be called,

Endurance, pain,
Their coaches' assurance 'No pain no gain!'

Forehands, backhands, chips,
Falls fury fiery words,

Is it all worth it? I hear them cry,
Suffering five sets in one single day!

The fans' favourite, the world's number 1,
Wimbledon - it's summer - on BBC 1.

David Gray (14)
The Rawlett School

Money!

Money, it's what I love and hate,
I like it when I can share it with a mate,
Money is really like a second god,
It buys me a good fishing rod.

But when I haven't got any money,
I'm always borrowing if off my buddy,
I can't buy anything without money,
Clothes, shoes or neither a tub of honey.

So money makes the world go round,
In my pocket I hope it's bound,
What I spend it on I don't really know,
It's probably on the money that I owe.

Ryan McKnight (14)
The Rawlett School

The River Of Change

The river in the valley was crystal clear,
Flowing gently like a sea of tears.
A captivating spectacle, close to my heart,
A place I warmed to, I couldn't depart.

In the spring he was warm, calm and asleep.
In the winter he was fierce, strong and deep.
I missed the river on the long winter days
Splashing against my feet in the nicest of ways

I longed for the time when my friend would return,
Until another winter, ferocious and stern.

Christopher Soult (14)
The Rawlett School

BULLYING

I see people being bullied,
In every sort of way,
I see people being bullied,
And there is nothing I can say.

I see people being bullied,
Being kicked and punched in the face,
I see people being bullied,
Mainly because of their race.

I see people being bullied,
And there is nothing I can do,
I see people being bullied,
Just tell me why and who?

I see people being bullied,
In every shape and sort,
I see people being bullied,
Can they not be taught?

I see people being bullied,
In every sort of way,
I see people being bullied,
And there is *something* I *can* say.

Jodie Reynolds (13)
The Rawlett School

WINTER

As the flakes of snow settle outside,
They turn the world a brilliant white.
A crisp icy sheet, sent by the frost,
Calls all nature, to a halt.

The streams and rivers stop their flow,
As they are frozen, to glittering glass.
The birds are called, by the south's warmth,
Leaving their homes and this land of white.

Although the animals have sheltered,
The aliveness of noise, is not all lost.
Children's joyful cheers show their delight,
As, yet another snowball whizzes by.

As the chills sends the children home,
Silence falls, once again,
While the snow still settles softly,
The world of white, gently sleeps.

Lucy Adams (13)
The Rawlett School

WILL YOU TELL ME THIS?

Will you tell me this . . .
  . . . Why does our world always look dull,
Showing the evils of criminals,
Giving us heartache and troublesome nights,
Asking ourselves, why?

Will you tell me this . . .
  . . . Why does bread land butter side down,
Leaving mess all over the floor,
Butter, jam and what not wasted,
Asking ourselves, why?

Will you tell me this . . .
. . . Why do all problems come at once,
Leaving us high and dry,
Disastrous worries all about nothing,
Asking ourselves, why?

Kate Bramwell (13)
The Rawlett School

MOURNING

As I stand here,
Watching over you all,
I think of everyone,
My parents and my wife and that baby so small.

You cannot see me,
But I can see you,
You cannot hear me,
But I hear you.

As I see my friends,
Sad and starting to cry,
I ask them to stop,
Do not mourn as I did not die.

As I am here watching over my friends,
Do not think the worse as I was not killed,
But think of the good times,
And now I must be going to another world.

Gary Thomas (13)
The Rawlett School

Why Me?

Why me, what have I done?
All I was doing was having some fun.
I was happy, really high,
I never thought that I could die.
All I took was the one
One minute I was here, then I was gone.
There was nothing the doctors could do anymore
All my parents' hopes of recovery were ripped and tore.
All they did was sit and cry.
Why couldn't I be saved? Why must I die?
My funeral was depressing and very sad
My mum cried and so did my dad.
Now that all is said and done
My life has ended and death has begun.

Nicholas Malone (13)
The Rawlett School

The Pool
(Natural v Artificial)

The pool, a desolate pit of water;
A cascade of raging torrents.
The pool, a natural smelling lake;
A smell of man-made substance.
The pool, a place of peace and quiet;
A realm of voice and laughter.
The pool, a natural quiet place;
A man-made humble home.
The pool, of clear limpid water;
A place of grit and grime.
The pool that lives, a pool that moves;
A pool that's dead is still.

James Dowen (13)
The Rawlett School

THE SEASONS

In spring little lambs are born,
And all old sheep are usually shorn,
Little baby chicks arrive,
And Jesus is declared alive,
Little birds tweet in the sky,
And we all stop eating mince pies.

In summer time the sun beats down,
O'er all the world, it's hot dry ground,
Everyone going to the sea,
Look carefully and you just might see,
France or Greece or Crete or Spain,
Summer's at an end again.

In autumn time the leaves are wet,
They have not been collected yet,
Children kick through piles of leaves,
That have long since fallen from the trees,
No-one knows just where to go,
During autumn, we hate it so.

You're never warned the day before,
It's winter time when you open the door,
And during winter time we go,
Through the fields of pure white snow,
Adults singing 'Deck the hall'
While children throw a small snowball.

So that's the story of the endless round,
Round and round and round and round,
So aren't you glad that you found,
This story of the endless round,
That never stops going round,
Round and round and round and round.

Emma Cardinal (13)
The Rawlett School

CHRISTMAS TIME

This Christmas Time people will be hungry,
And some of them won't have a bed,
They will not have a family to love
They won't have a roof over their head.

This Christmas Time, some children will not
    receive gifts,
There are people who won't have a tree,
There are people who will not have happiness,
They won't be as lucky as me.

So when the time comes for this Christmas,
We should think of the people who are poor,
The people who will not have love in their lives,
The people who don't have a front door.

Louise Hicks (13)
The Rawlett School

CHANGING SEPTEMBER

September is a month of change
Where the young man, who is summer,
Who is lively and cheerful, colourful and bright,
Changes to the middle-aged man of autumn
Who sits on a throne of golden corn,
Waiting for the cold and dying winter to come.

In September birds nestle
In the canopy of green trees,
Which make man September's hair.
When he starts to lose his green locks
He too loses some of the birds that used to live there.
Once man September's birds and locks
Have gone, he feels bare like a bald old man.

Russell Inglis (12)
The Rawlett School

WINTRY OCTOBER

An old extraordinary man,
Walking very slowly, glancing as he goes,
With a sparkle in his bloodshot eyes
And the glow of his shining rosy red cheeks.
He is wearing dark dingy colours
Brown, black, not a pastel colour in sight.
He looks like a happy man
With a smile on his wrinkled old face.

Home he goes, to and fro
To a roaring coal fire
As bright as the stars can go,
As he sits in his nice warm chair
With a steaming hot cup of cocoa,
He looks and sees leaves come off the trees
With the strong howling winds.

Shelley Anderton (11)
The Rawlett School

THE DALES

As I wandered slowly through the Yorkshire dales,
Past rushing rivers and gorges deep,
My mind escaped to ages past,
When melting ice littered the landscape with
Boulders large and small,
And men eked out their meagre
Lives in caves deep and dark,
When woolly mammoths roamed at large
And bears skulked in caves.
Now, as then,
The sun sank in the west and
Thoughts turned to the new day.

Kieran Eason (13)
The Rawlett School

THE ROAD IS OUR GRAVEYARD

The road is our graveyard,
The place where we die,
Where tyres hit us hard,
As your car goes by.

You do not see us,
You take no heed,
Just go up a gear,
To increase your speed.

We may be a badger,
We may be a fox,
But we are not buried,
In a long, black box.

We lie there in pain,
Knowing that soon,
We will meet our end,
In the night's long gloom.

Then there we are left,
And there we shall stay,
Until in time,
We will rot away.

Sarah Jellema (13)
The Rawlett School

Old Winter

A wrinkled, rugged man I picture here,
Old fellow with eyes as bright as stars,
Red lips, as red as a drop of blood,
Plodding along through the slush and ice.

Old winter walking down the cobbled street,
Watching children at their happiest,
Tightly wrapped in a coat of wool,
Old winter,

Holly bushes all around,
With scarlet berries and all,
Old winter,
Plodding along once more.

Anna Read (11)
The Rawlett School

Snow Man

Snow is falling very fast,
It starts to settle on the grass,
When it stops I'll go outside,
And start to make a snowman.

Snow it sticks quite fast,
My snowman's almost finished,
The snow melts fast in my hand,
I'll go back in to fetch my gloves.

Snow, it's starting to melt,
Now I've finished at last,
Just the pipe to go in his mouth,
I then just watch him melt.

Ben Wilkins (11)
The Rawlett School

LEAP TO FEBRUARY

You only see him every four years,
with scaly skin and a frosty beard,
His fingers are like icicles to touch,
There's a foggy mist around him,
I don't think I like him very much.

If you catch him smiling,
You will see a ray of sun,
It doesn't last for very long,
There's not much time for fun,
Before he pulls his dark black cloak around him,
And night time has begun.

Although he's only short,
He can be dangerous,
Leaving behind coughs and colds,
Children must be told
Look before you *leap*.

Dale Lomas (11)
The Rawlett School

BLIND GIRL

She can only see from her mind,
See pictures that are in the wind,
Her voice should have been dear,
To her mothers own ear,
She could hardly speak,
As she was so weak.

It must be such a pain,
Almost like being on a chain,
She was very meek,
Yet every week,
Out loud she would cry.
That she wanted to die

Her life shouldn't have been like this,
Should not have been hell but bliss,
Yet people say still,
You can hear her cries on top of
The hill.

Katie Logan (13)
The Rawlett School

END OF MY WORLD

As I walk people are dying,
The conditions are dirty and some disgusting,
My world is falling apart.

Everything is covered in flies and dust,
The echoing cries of agony,
My world is falling apart.

My fight for life goes on,
People's fight for good continues,
My world is falling apart.

I drop to my knees as I get weaker,
I take a deep breath, but all I breathe is dust and dead air,
My world is falling apart.

I lie myself down and put myself to rest,
Now I know I can join my brother,
My world has fallen apart.

Gregg Sadler (13)
The Rawlett School

Two Crazy Scots

On Sunday we came back from Devon
After having three days away.
The ice-creams, fudge and pasties
Almost made me want to stay.

Arriving home gave me a thought:
Mum's friends were coming that day
And I'd still got some homework to do
But I knew what she would say.

'Why didn't you do it earlier?
Kay and Jim are here now.'
'I don't know what to write about
A football, a man or a cow!'

Kay and Jim were from Scotland
And they started to talk to me,
They asked me if I'd done my homework
So I thought then said 'Mostly.'

'I've still got to write a poem
But based on goodness knows what.'
'Well why don't you write your poem
About us two crazy Scots!'

Fiona McGown (13)
The Rawlett School

THE DATE

Ribbons in my hair,
Rouge on my lips,
Soon we'll be eating,
Caviar and chips.

Walk down the road,
Hand in hand,
Dancing to the beat,
Of a pop band.

Me dressed all pretty,
Him dressed in a suit,
Him wearing trainers,
Me wearing high heeled boots,

He'll soon be here,
He's coming at eight,
I'm so excited,
We're going on a date,

He walks in the door,
Says 'Hello Jean,'
I fall on the floor
He's wearing a Man U shirt and jeans!

Laura Hunt (11)
The Rawlett School

FOOTBALL

Running, sprinting, with the ball,
Past the players preparing to score,
Step back, breathe in, and shoot,
It's a goal!

Celebrate with the team,
Then it's kick off again,
This time they're coming at us,
Polly whacks it away,
I run onto the ball,
I've just been fouled.

It's my penalty now and I run,
I shoot, it hits the post,
It rebounds, Andrea whacks it in the net
Goal!
Then the whistle blows
It's full time
What a game!

Heather Smith (11)
The Rawlett School

THE MATCH

The roar of the crowd,
One man shouts aloud
Handball, handball, handball,
But the referee waves play on because for now he
controls them all.

The little number 8 takes on one, two, three, now four and
has only the keeper to beat,
The player is still running and can feel the tension and heat,
As he gets closer and closer he can see his opponent leap,
crash, bang, wallop, this great run ends in a heap.

The whistle is blown for a peno he can't believe his luck,
His opponent is red carded and waddles off like a duck,
The kick is taken and the ball flies through the air,
The ball lands in the net, the opposite fans know it's
over and shout and go spare.

Matthew Hunt (13)
The Rawlett School

NOTHING TO GAIN AND NOTHING TO GIVE
(A response to Timothy Winters by Charles Causley)

A child is born with no state of mind,
Blind to the ways of mankind,
No state of duty. No life to live,
Nothing to gain and nothing to give.

His parents don't care about him too much,
His mom's too drunk and his dad is too butch.
No friends at school, no friends at home
No friends to trust: he's all on his own.

The kids at his school say, 'What's that stink!'
But how can he wash, when he hasn't a sink?
With just one pair of clothes for school,
His others are hand-downs: all too small.

But he will go on, he will grow up,
Fighting life's problems, longing for luck.
No education, no life to live.
Nothing to gain. Nothing to give.

Dan Thompson (12)
The Rawlett School

FOOTBALL

Football is a passionate game,
Which has brought stars their brilliant fame,
It is a game in which you kick a ball,
Many think it's ace and many think it's cool.

It causes many injuries,
It causes many fights,
It's a part of the game where the referee bites,

He either cautions or even sends off,
He rolls his eyes and gives a little cough,
The players walk off with great shame,
They are sad that they can't play the game.

The managers are about to blow a fuse,
It's the referee that they mainly accuse,
The assistants try to calm them down,
The managers walk off with an abusive frown.

The players walk to the penalty spot,
The opposition feel as they've been shot,
The players step two paces away,
Thank goodness there hasn't been a fray,
The player stares at the timid keeper,
He looks back a little sheeper
The penalty has been taken with great power,

We all hope that it doesn't turn sour,
We have won the cup that is really great,
For the other team that is their fate,
The opposition look on and disapprove,
Their only wish is that they want to improve.

Luke Woollard (13)
The Rawlett School

THIS DREAM

There was a time,
We thought our dream was over,
When you and I had surely reached the end,
Still here we are,
The flame as strong as ever,
All because we both kept holding on,

As time goes by, we've learnt to rediscover,
The reason why,
This dream of ours survives,
Through thick and thin,
We're destined for each other,
Knowing we can reach the other side,
Far beyond the mountains of our pride.

I said a lot of things,
A lot of things I didn't mean to say,
I never meant to hurt you,
I was wrong to fight with you that way,
But I'm only human,
I let my pride deceive me,
You're the lover I need in my life,
If you still don't believe me.

Nadeem Hussain (15)
The Rawlett School

My Nana (Davis)

My Nan was such a nice lady
She had a heart of gold
This we all knew
And were so often told.

We never left your side
You lay there chatting away
Never grumbling or moaning
Did you know this was your last day?

You looked so comfortable and healthy
Then you slipped away
But we will meet again
I know we will one day.

Juanita Chatterton (15)
Trent Valley High School

Casey's Recipe Poem

Open 14 year old girl from bedding,
Gently immerse in saucepan of soap and simmer for 3 minutes
Sprinkle with dash of deodorant,
Set grill to four sitting around table,
Heat slowly until piping hot throughout,
Add ounce of moody brother,
Spread sleepiness slightly over the top
Bring mother to the boil,
Add tablespoon of attitude
Reheat to a temperature of a boiling father
Cool off with a slow walk to school
Lightly season with homework
Best served with dash of romance.

Casey Wakeman (14)
Trent Valley High School

TODAY'S WORLD

Today's world has changed so quickly,
Babies being born,
Many of them die,
Mothers and fathers mourn,
Now the child has died so has the mild side
of the parents' life.

Toddlers running about,
Others crying for food and drink,
How many of these will live,
And how many will die,
Nobody knows only the world will find out about
this lie.

Parents worrying over nothing,
Child runs away,
Parents find another way to get them back,
Now they have found the child,
The child tells them to back off.

Old people who live in homes,
Don't have the freedom of this world,
Many feeling unhappy and alone,
Others just sit back alone and watch
the world go by.

Now tell me how does this world go on,
Children, parents and even grandparents the most,
Hate the fighting and squabbling,
Everyone rambling on and on,

Now answer me this 'Is this world a better place?'
Or could this world have a *big change*.

Zakia Khan (14)
Trent Valley High School

Racism

Every day's the same
I come to school
And all I hear are racist names.
Why is it me?
I've never done anything wrong
So why do they call me a black mong?
I try to ignore them
But it never does any good
Every day they grab me
And throw me in dirty mud.
I can't ignore them
It's just too much.
I never complain to the teachers
Because I know it'll do no good.
The teachers are all the same
They just ignore me even though they know
That I'm a victim of racism - how low!
I know the teachers will probably expel me
But that's just too big a risk to take
My parents are depending on me
I'm their only hope
But what can I do?
Life's not fair with me
But I can't complain.
There's no-one left who can help
Now my only hope is God
I hope he listens
I know he's always there.
Maybe there is a little hope
But I'll have to live my life to know.

Abda Liaget (14)
Trent Valley High School

DADDY'S GONE

I was just a little girl wrapped up in a dream world of ambitions,
Obsessed with teddy bears and daisy chains,
I did not know what was happening to us,
Suddenly I had been pulled, yanked out, out of my little world,
Was in a cold kitchen, with white walls and the smells of cooking,
Mum sat at the table, still and cold apprehensive I sat down too,
Yet deep down I knew, I knew,
I had already felt the pain,
I had seen it on the TV, in trashy soaps and sitcoms,
But I did not think that it was real,
Her eyes warm and loving towards us, yet if you looked deep
                                                                  inside to her soul,
There was anger, rage, betrayal, pain, sadness and numbness,
Her voice shook I stared,
I waited for the words to pour from her lips into my ears,
I wanted to muffle them, I did not want to hear the sounds,
It was like an eternity passed by in those seconds,
So many thoughts spinning around in my head,
I heard cars in the street,
Birds tweet and twitter in the garden,
The dogs barking but loudest of all my own heartbeat pounding out
                                                                   into the silence,
Then she said the words I knew I would hear,
'We are getting a divorce,'
I acted like I did not mind, that this meant nothing to me,
                                                                   I screamed, I cried,
But the strength I showed her seemed to overcome me,
I was no longer a little girl, now a social worker, counsellor,
And above all I needed the strength of a woman.

Elizabeth Finney (15)
Trent Valley High School

The Bungalow

I stood deserted, with boards all around,
Large, cruel weeds all over my ground,
No flowers around, no trees or shrubs,
Behind my walls were insects and grubs,

My cold corridors were dusty and dirty,
Not like when I was built in 1930,
My walls were weak, all cracking and crumbling,
My tall heavy chimneys soon would be tumbling,

But then someone bought me after eight years alone,
Since then I have blossomed, improved and grown,
My spacious rooms are inviting and clean,
No boards any more, I have windows that gleam,

My corridors are now furnished with pictures and lights,
My walls are strong and my rooms are light,
There's a patio now, with a lovely big pond,
At last I am lived in, of me they are fond.

Jacqueline Beeston (13)
Trent Valley High School

Recipe For Samantha Eldridge

Take one very enigmatic teenager,
And add a pinch of confidence
Season with intelligence and charm
And bring to the boil at a late night party.

Wake at 7am for school
Add gel to hair and comb through
Garnish with hairspray
Then lightly spread with make-up.

Sprinkle with clothes and jewellery
Spice up with a little perfume
Fill with cereals and lashings of toast
Spoon mixture into car and drive to school
Then allow to simmer for the remainder of the day.

Samantha Eldridge (14)
Trent Valley High School

AIR RAID

I hear the sirens,
I hear the planes,
I rush into the deep, dark shelter.
There I wait.
I hear the droning planes,
The screaming of bombs,
Dropping to the ground.

I hear the sirens,
I hear the birds,
I rush into the house,
Up into my warm, light room.
There I wait.
I hear the singing of birds,
The chirping of blue-tits,
Swooping to the ground,
Because peace is finally here.

Matthew Oakes (11)
Trentham High School

THE WIND

The wind sweeps through the sky, dancing without
a care in the world,
It can be strong or just a cool gentle breeze,
Amazing either way,
We ask the wind show yourself wherever you are,
You are stronger than rain,
More amazing than the sun,
Helpful and kind,
Dangerous at times,
How strong can you blow?
As you blow you whistle to me, you
swerve gracefully through the windows,
When I go out I pull on my gloves,
and tie my scarf,
I feel you freezing my nose and make it,
glow rosy red, but I still love you.

Suzanne Byatt (13)
Trentham High School

THE SUNSET

The sunset on the horizon,
As beautiful as can be,
The dazzling colours of the sun,
In the gentle summer breeze,
The day is almost over,
The evening's just begun,
I'll sit awhile and ponder,
In the early evening sun.

Laura Beckett (12)
Trentham High School

HAVE YOU EVER WONDERED...?

Have you ever wondered
What God, up there, should be?
Is *he* a *her*?
Or is *she* a *he*.

Is he a giant human?
Or a microscopic fly?
Is he a poor old beggar
Who's struggling to get by?

With all of God's creations
He's as rich as should come.
I'll bet that every night he drinks
Pure old Jamaican rum.

Is he nasty to the angels,
And bosses them about?
Does he smack poor Jesus on his bum?
(Now that I very much doubt!)

No, God is kind and loving
And a father to us all.
And we shouldn't wonder
Whether he's fat, short, thin or tall.

Felicity Clarke (13)
Trentham High School

AT THE DEAD OF NIGHT

The fox comes out
                at the dead of night
There is no-one around
                there is no light
He seizes his chance
                and darts over the field
Hoping he's not seen
                as a fox has no shield
This time he is lucky
                he gets there with no fight
Tomorrow it could all change
                at the dead of night.

Zara Kassai (12)
Trentham High School

FAIRGROUND

Lights and music waking you up,
Looking out the window dying for a look,
Rides and food with lights galore.
Waltzes and big wheel looking for more
Run downstairs see even more,
Ghost trains, and the heartbreaker,
Rides you adore,
Children with candyfloss, and lots of small rides,
Go in to the spooky house what a surprise,
Wish I could be there with all the rides
Maybe mum will let me when I turn five.

Katie Williams (13)
Weston Road High School

BETRAYED

A holiday romance led to something more.
A friendship that would last,
A pen-pal from far away,
To tell what's in the past.

The letters stopped suddenly
My heart its sadness shone.
But then a letter finally came
Jonathan was gone!

He died in a train crash,
About two years ago
If I dare to stop and think,
I know I'll miss him so.

The every thought of sadness
That is risen from the train
The loss, the cold, the emptiness
And the cries and shrieks of pain.

If I stop to imagine
I can't bear to try,
To be so happy but then so sad
He would not have time to cry.

When at last I stopped believing
My life would be the same
For the loss of Jonathan
Flows through me again and again.

Joanne Emery (13)
Weston Road High School

DON'T BE CRUEL TO ANIMALS

Don't be cruel to animals,
Or tie them to a chain
And make them perform to people
Which causes lots of pain.

Who needs elephant's ivory,
To play a game of chess
And if we could stop it happening,
It would be a great success!

Emily Garner (11)
Weston Road High School

I CAN'T UNDERSTAND

Is snow really snow?
Is land really land?
Does anyone know?
Can you understand?

It's just a bit of stuff
lying on the ground.
Is the world really round?
Why does it move without
making a sound?
These are all questions that
answers can't be found.

Stephanie Wheat (11)
Weston Road High School

WHEN OLD AGE TAKES OVER

When old age takes over my body,
What will I be like?
An eccentric loner,
A gibbering idiot,
A loved mother,
Or an older version of this innocent child?

When my brown locks turn grey,
What will I look alike?
Dull and lifeless,
A dribbling fool,
Or a thoughtful, cheerful woman?

When death is knocking at my door,
What will I feel like?
Scared and lonely,
Glad to be rid of pain,
Will I fight to the end,
Or bravely meet my maker?

When God is standing over me,
What will he see?
A selfish waster,
A cold heartless being,
A saint,
Or the real me?

Lisa Baskeville (16)
Weston Road High School

ALONE WITH MY THOUGHTS

Sitting in the grass,
Staring at the stars,
Looking back in time,
Maybe a million years.

>My mind is always blown
>As I try to imagine
>Just how large the Universe is
>And what a significant part.

>>A simple person, like
>>You or me, plays in it.
>>Eternity is hard to imagine,
>>Maybe I should just quit. But

I often let my thoughts control me
As I sit and think,
Glancing at the stars
With nothing at all to do but

>*Think!*

Kathryn Baldwin (15)
Weston Road High School

GUITARS

Guitars are wicked,
Guitars are loud,
If you play 'em loud enough,
You can touch the clouds.

You play 'em with pride,
You play 'em with joy,
They aren't for girls,
They're just for boys.

Guitars are brilliant,
Guitars are ace,
You can play 'em,
In any place.

Guitars are good,
Guitars are cool,
Play 'em at home,
Or in a pool.

Paul Hayward (12)
Weston Road High School

UNTITLED

I feel like I'm flying,
over an angry hell,
I feel like crying,
but someone might tell,
I'm scared to death,
I hope that's not true,
I'm in a mess,
I don't know what to do,
There's fire and tears,
Burning inside me,
Anger and fears,
Like in the cold sea,
My emotions are swirling
Around and around,
I'm falling, falling,
Down to the ground.

Rachel Ward (14)
Weston Road High School

STANDING IN YOUR SHADOW

If you ever need someone,
I'll be there,
Standing in your shadow.
If you ever need a shoulder to cry on,
I'll be there,
Standing in your shadow.
If you are ever alone,
I'll be there,
Standing in your shadow.
If you ever forget me,
I'll be there,
Standing in your shadow.

Tamsine Bellaby (16)
Weston Road High School

TRAPPED

Trapped
In infinity,
Forever wandering,
Searching,
For what?
Forever finding,
Never knowing,
Still searching,
For nothing,
No sound,
Or emotion,
Just trapped
In infinity . . .

Kylie Godridge (14)
Weston Road High School

SHINING SEA

The sea is glowing,
Glowing gold,
The wind is blowing,
Blowing cold,
And I am growing,
Growing old,
As I sit here by the sea.

I've sat here for a hundred years,
Shedding no fears,
Shedding no tears,
But as I sit here by the sea,
What future is there?
What future for me?

Grace Elkin (12)
Weston Road High School

MY FAMILY

I have a little brother
His hair is very red,
He has a lot of freckles
and he talks in bed

I have another brother
but he's the older one
and when he's in a good mood
he can be rather fun.

I have a little sister
she is just, the best
although she's cute and cuddly
she can be quite a pest.

Ben Doyle (12)
Weston Road High School

MENDED WITH GLUE

You broke my heart, but I mended it with glue.
Mist outside won't hide the green glow of your eyes.
My personal pain in the neck is you,
But I forgive you for your mishaps and lies.
I'd show you how I feel but I am dumb.
It's not all my fault, you can take the blame
In bed without you, I feel numb.
Burn me with your hot fire, not dead ash of your shame.
Give some love, take my empty heart to fill,
I am doll parts, not gutless, not heartless.
I'd commit suicide, for you I would kill
Yin-Yang, love - hate, innocent - guilty, me and you,
Evian water-battery acid, our love is so true.

Gemma Allen (15)
Weston Road High Schoo

LIFE

I walked through the corridor of life
Trying to find my destiny
I saw a light at the end
I felt a silence
The water stopped dripping from the walls
I was scared
I tried to run back but it went on and on
I couldn't get out
I was trapped
It was then I found my life
In a graveyard
I was alone.

Sarah Dellar (13)
Weston Road High School

I STOP . . .

I crawl through the door,
I stop . . . and wait,
for a head to turn against me.

I turn to my left,
walk six paces, I stop . . .
and sit down in an
abandoned chair, alone, silently.

In the noise of the room
I silently open my bag,
and present a book to myself.
I stop (although content with my emotions)
and look cautiously around for friendship,
I stop . . . and wait,
for a head to turn against me,
                         Nothing, silence!

I continue moving my head back to the book,
and stop . . .
I read to my heart's content aloud,
waiting for a head to turn towards me,

I stop . . .

Jason Howard (16)
Weston Road High School

Mum And Dad

Mum and Dad
Met a long time ago
Their friendship came fast
Though their courtship was slow.

They love each other dearly
They'll never come to part
I knew this very fact
Right from the start.

Mum got married in a beautiful cream dress
She was very nervous
through wedding day stress.

Dad wore a suit,
and a bright red tie
He looks upon it now
with a huge big sigh.

About five years later
I came on the scene
beautiful and sweet
like peaches and cream

I look at pictures now
hating what I see
My family don't agree with this
They say I'm a sweet pea.

My brother came along
With beautiful big brown eyes
A head of fiery red
Boy what a surprise.

A few years later
seventeen to be exact
Dad's a little balder
and mum's a little fat.

Now my brother's eight years old
and all is going well
Though mum and dad
Sometimes call it hell.

Abigail Cheshire (12)
Weston Road High School

MINDLESS ECHO

I hear an echo going round,
        Without a murmur
there was no sound.
The shadows of silence began to fall,
        as I was walking down
the echoless hall.
A prism of light fell on the
windowpane,
        the path of light
was born again
The sound of silence began to fade,
        The sound of music
Outside was made.
I left the darkness into light,
        The inside world
Still held my fright.
Now daytime is falling into night,
But soon enough it will be light.

Philippa Valler (15)
Weston Road High School

The Lonely Tiger

Its eyes staring grimly, its nose soft and wet.
Its shoulders are laid back, and its tail is set,
as the lonely tiger strolls along, its eyes staring,
I watched it closely its eyes glaring, glaring,
glaring.
You could see it was lonely,
as it walks in its figure of eight.
I would love to set it free,
but I think it's too late.

Jemma Sellers (12)
Windsor Park Middle School

The Bear

He comes from afar in a cooped up cage,
Not able to hunt,
Not able to move.

He comes from afar in a cooped up cage,
Not knowing his destination,
Forgetting his destiny.

He comes from afar in a cooped up cage,
His whiskers are bent and ragged,
His tongue is as dry as desert sands.

He comes from afar in a cooped up cage,
His destination: the zoo.

Ashley Roe (12)
Windsor Park Middle School

THE ROMAN SOLDIER

The Roman soldier,
Standing in the shadows,
Lonely, dusty and cold.
The sun's light shines on everything,
Except the poor, lonely soldier.
Waiting to be free,
Free into the light,
And free from the dust.

Andrew Woodings (12)
Windsor Park Middle School

BIG TEDDY

Big teddy just seems to lie there,
Locked in the cupboard looking as if he's
thinking thoughtfully.
Staring at the floor with his one eye,
The other one is somewhere . . . in Manchester!
He used to have a bib, but that was chewed
off,
He used to have white arms that are now
brown with dirt.
He has pink hands on his brown arms,
Reminding me of strawberry ice-cream,
left to melt.
As time goes on, he sits there, collecting dust.
I could throw him away, but I don't think I will,
He means too much to me.

Nadia Nijim (12)
Windsor Park Middle School

BEING SMALL

It was hell,
Being small isn't easy.
My stomach churned,
My heart burned,
Every day was another burden,
Every day I held my tongue,
I felt weak, helpless.
My stomach churned,
My heart burned,
Their cruel faces
And sharp scissor mouths.
I was in a cage,
A worthless feeling took over me,
I couldn't get out.
My stomach churned,
My heart burned,
Until the day I told.
The teachers helped,
The bullies yelped,
They cried and called me a liar,
But at last the fight was over.

Helen Crump (12)
Windsor Park Middle School

TIGER'S HELL

Lonely does the tiger live,
staring out at a nearby antelope,
also trapped in a cage.

In the pouring rain it sits,
as if it is made from stone,
small shrubs and patchy grass is this
tiger's home.

Watched intently by small children,
the tiger stands as if it is on show,
like a fashion model parading up and down.

In the hot sun the tiger searches for shade,
but instead finds none.
The hot and bothered tiger continues its
hellish life.

James Brazendale (12)
Windsor Park Middle School

A BAD DAY AT SCHOOL

Why did the teacher tell me off
When all I did was find the page in the
book we were reading?
When I was late coming off the
playground,
I had to write one hundred times,
'I must get in school on time,
I must get in school on time'.

When a rubber is thrown in class,
where does it land?
Nowhere other than in my eye.
At lunch, when I eat my chocolate bar,
Someone has to come and knock it
onto the floor.
Then in my final lesson that day, I
found out,
I got a 'C-' for my homework.

Sometimes school just isn't fair!

Caroline Williams (12)
Windsor Park Middle School

1st Deep

Decide the positions for the rounders match,
I get 1st deep where you don't have to catch,
'I think I'm a good catcher' I always have to protest.
'Yeah but you're not as good as some of the best.'

I go to my place and pick up a daisy
'Come on 1st deep, stop being so lazy.'
I stand and watch the other team scoring,
Being 1st deep is just so boring.

'Oh stop moaning and get ready to run.'
Being 1st deep is just not fun.
'She's hit it hard, 1st deep get running.'
I wake up suddenly and the ball's coming, *it's coming?*

'Oh look at her run. She's gonna blow it,
Why don't we replace her with someone who can throw it!'
I've got to throw it straight at 4th post,
To stop the other team from scoring the most.

I grab the ball and throw it hard,
I must have thrown it a million yards.
Our captain cheers as she does a great leap
'Next time someone else can be 1st deep!'

Justine Locker (12)
Windsor Park Middle School

THE SWIMMING RACE

Start block,
Gun fires,
High dive,
Long glide,
Start stroke,
Good pace,
First turn,
Gone well,
Knees kicking,
Arms pumping,
Gasping breaths,
Mind focused,
Second place,
Turn approaching,
Slipped up,
Dropped back,
Fourth place,
Trying harder,
Last turn,
Moved up,
Third place,
Strong battle,
Going faster,
Arms numb,
Legs tired,
Super sprint,
Finished now,
Feel brill,
Came first,
Gold mine.

Graham Langridge (12)
Windsor Park Middle School

Swimming Gala

Hello and welcome to our annual swimming gala
Being held in Frederick Water's back garden.
With your favourite commentator George Wash.
The pool looks in superb condition.
And I think they're starting to go up to the line
for their dive.
Bang they're off,
And in first place it's Jimmy Go.
In second place it's Steve Wet,
and in . . .
Oh yes Steve Wet has gone into first place.
And now in third place it's Mick Soap,
In fourth place it's . . .
Oh no!
Jimmy Go is disqualified for wetting his mum
And in fourth place it's Frederick Water
And Oh my God Frederick is catching up with
Mick Soap
And Frederick has overtaken Mick
And Mick has got out of the pool
And he's gone home for his tea.
Now they're coming up to the last corner
And it's Steve Wet in first place
Frederick Water in second place
And Jimmy Go in third place
And Mick Soap in fourth place.
This is George Wash handing you back to the
Studio.

Steven Kerry (12)
Windsor Park Middle School

LAMPSHADE

Last year I never went out at breaks,
I was scared of what would happen.
People used to tug my hair and say it was a 'lampshade'.
I also got called 'mushroom' and 'cycle helmet'.
At first I hated it and once I even cried.
I thought they would tug out clumps of hair,
Thank goodness they never did!
I told my Mum and she just laughed,
When I told my Dad he laughed too.
And now I see the funny side,
But I still don't go out at breaks.

Helen Wilson (12)
Windsor Park Middle School

A LETTER

This is a letter from me to you,
A letter, a message, a word or two,
A way of passing information from A to B
A way to express my feelings completely.

A letter is media like none of the others,
I won't tell of war or of royal lovers,
I won't tell of a mad cow or even a mad pig,
I have no big story and the scandal isn't big.

In this letter I can tell you if I'm happy or sad,
I can tell you if I'm angry or glad.
This is a genuine letter from me to you,
A letter, a message, a word or two.

Connie Corbishley (13)
Windsor Park Middle School

SPECKIE FOUR EYES

'Speckie four eyes. Double glazing,'
Two mean boys shouted across the playground at me.
The sun was shining like a crystal in the sky.
'I'm not,' I repeated over and over again.
'Speckie four eyes. Double glazing.'
They were now standing next to me.
'What have I done to be treated like this?' I asked.
'You haven't done anything we're just bored.'
'Speckie four eyes. Double glazing.
If you dob we'll smash your glasses.'
By now I had tears streaming down my face.
They walked off chanting
'Speckie four eyes. Double glazing.'
I sat in the corner sobbing
I thought and thought
Until I had no choice.
I had to tell.

Hayley Goodwin (12)
Windsor Park Middle School

YELLOW

Yellow is a daffodil waving
in the midday breeze.
Yellow is the sun, shining
on a hot summer's day,
rabbits eating dandelions
while running in the garden.
Yellow is the colour of
banana ice-cream
and children using yellow
crayons to finish off a picture.

Kelly Staley (12)
Windsor Park Middle School

WHEN I WAS BULLIED

When I was bullied,
Terror ran over my face,
And everyone around me,
Just laughed and said 'You weed!'

I didn't ever tell,
'Cause fear took over me.
After that I got called names,
And I just couldn't cope.

But now I know,
When to tell a teacher or friend,
Anyway I don't get bullied now,
Because I told.

Andrew Aitken (12)
Windsor Park Middle School

TENNIS!

Tennis time is here once more,
I can't get my mother out of the door,
She sits in a chair by the TV,
And when the tennis is on she ignores me.

For two whole weeks she's glued to the set,
She watches intensely as the ball hits the net,
Her head moves from side to side
As 'Game, set and match,' the umpire cried.

After two whole weeks the time has passed,
My mother's favourite player always comes last.
Thank goodness Wimbledon is at an end,
Perhaps my mum will now be my friend.

Lyndi Thompson (12)
Windsor Park Middle School

NOTHING EVER HAPPENS

Nothing ever happens,
Every day is the same.
The same old Stevenson's bus,
Same route, same stops, same passengers,
The driver never speaks,
He just looks at you in a funny way.

Nothing ever happens,
The classroom has not changed,
I put my coat on the same peg,
talk to the same friends,
say the same things,
Then the bell goes.

Nothing ever happens,
Registration is always the same.
Teacher calls out the names,
in the same order,
Nobody says anything but 'Yes Miss'
Then it is assembly time.

Nothing ever happens,
We sit in the same places,
Five hundred blank expressions,
The teacher drones on.
We sing a boring hymn in a boring way,
Then we go to our class.

Nothing ever happens,
We do the same exercises,
We learn the same things,
Before and after break,
Before and after lunch,
day after day after day.

One day I will go to school by
spaceship,
My green skin will startle my friends,
I will shout 'No Miss I'm not here,'
And dance on the stage.
Then something will happen.

Kate Backhouse (12)
Windsor Park Middle School

THE ME I USED TO BE

Look at that dress,
It doesn't fit me now
And look at those socks,
They're too short for me somehow.
Look at my hair,
It's a mess on there,
How could I dress like that?
I suppose it was the only way I knew,
How to be me.

Sarah Turner (13)
Windsor Park Middle School

TV Ads

Aquafresh - not just a pretty paste,
Doublemint's got a fresh minty taste,
But does that make up for the stupid ad
Which shows a woman whose breath is bad?
These hair product ads are so over the top,
You're not told that VO5 makes your hair like a mop!
If you drink Rio when you're on a plane,
You can make the whole of the crew go insane!
They'll dance about in an African fashion,
I really hate that ad with a passion.
Talking dogs asking for their tea?
That's just ridiculous if you ask me.
And what about the red phone that beeps?
If you need insurance he'll be by your feet,
How does it move and make that noise?
I've seen better kiddies' toys!
And why would you shave your legs in a lift?
Or buy dad a spanner as a Christmas gift?

Although I hate ads what would I do?
If there wasn't that break to rush to the loo?
I couldn't get food and I'd starve to death,
And as I drew my very last breath,
I'd pray to God for TV ads,
'Cause after all, they're not that bad!

Vicky Bailey (13)
Windsor Park Middle School

INFORMATION

We hope you have enjoyed reading this book - and that you will continue to enjoy it in the coming years.

If you like reading and writing poetry drop us a line, or give us a call, and we'll send you a free information pack.

Write to :-

**Young Writers Information
1-2 Wainman Road
Woodston
Peterborough
PE2 7BU**